HUMMINGBIRDS OF THE CARIBBEAN

HUMMINGBIRDS OF THE CARIBBEAN

Text by Esther Quesada Tyrrell

Photographs by Robert A. Tyrrell

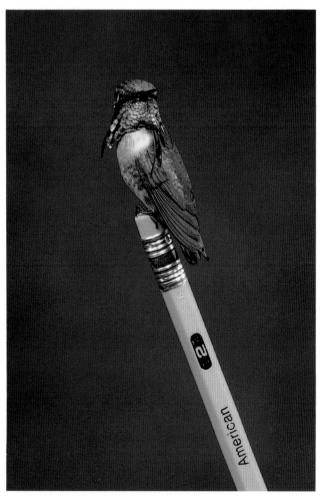

Male Bee Hummingbird, the smallest bird in the world. Shown life-size.

Crown Publishers, Inc., New York

Anatomical rendering of tongue, skeleton, nuptial dive of Bee Hummingbird, aggression display of Bee Hummingbird, copulation of Vervain Hummingbird, and comparison of hummingbird/pelican/man wing bones copyright © by D. DeGrazia.

Drawings of mites copyright © by S. Naeem.

Comparison of sizes of birds Artist Ad Cameron copyright © by Equinox (Oxford) Limited

Hummingbird zemi from *The Aborigines of Puerto Rico and neighboring islands* by J. W. Fewkes, 25th Annual Report, Bureau of American Ethnology, Smithsonian Institution, Washington, D.C., 1907.

Flight display of the Vervain Hummingbird copyright © 1967 Gosse Bird Club. 8:13.

Songs, calls, courtship displays, and copulation of Western and Eastern Streamertails, courtship display of the Antillean Crested Hummingbird, and songs, courtship display, and copulation of the Purple-throated Carib copyright reprinted by permission of Karl-L. Schuchmann.

Drawing of hummingbird heads and flowers reprinted by permission of Ecological Society of America.

Drawing of hummingbird bills from "The Hummingbirds," *Report of the U.S. National Museum for 1890,* by R. Ridgway.

Descriptions of each species after "The Birds of North and Middle America." Part V. *Bulletin of the U.S. National Museum.* 1911, by R. Ridgway.

Spectrograms of the vocalizations of the male Bee Hummingbird copyright © 1989 by George Reynard.

Hummingbird fan provided by the Fine Arts Museums of San Francisco. Gift of Mrs. Carrie Benson Mitchell. Accession no. 50873, 1880.

Photograph of James Bond courtesy of the Academy of Natural Sciences, Philadelphia.
Photograph of Dr. Harold Edgerton courtesy Dr. Harold Edgerton.

Published by Crown Publishers, Inc., 201 East 50th Street, New York, New York 10022

CROWN is a trademark of Crown Publishers, Inc.

Manufactured in Japan

Library of Congress Cataloging-in-Publication Data
Tyrrell, Esther Quesada.
Hummingbirds of the Caribbean, their life and behavior: a portfolio of the Caribbean species/text by Esther Quesada Tyrrell; photographs by Robert A. Tyrrell.
p.   cm.
Bibliography: p.
Includes index.
1. Hummingbirds—Caribbean Area.   I. Tyrrell, Robert A.   II. Title
QL696.A558T86   1990
598.8'99—dc20   89-7656
ISBN 0-517-57368-7

1   3   5   7   9   10   8   6   4   2

First Edition

We dedicate our book to the following two men whose notable achievements have left an impressive legacy in their respective fields. Each one generously shared his expertise with us and helped make this book possible.

James Bond
(1900–1989)
Curator of Ornithology Emeritus
Academy of Natural Sciences of Philadelphia

Beginning in 1926, James Bond devoted himself to the study of the birds of the West Indies. In 1933, he publicly stated his theory that the birds of that region were North American in origin, not South American, as was widely believed. Although his theory met with considerable skepticism from the scientific community (who clung to their views despite the fact that there was no critical evidence to support them), today it is widely held that he was, indeed, correct.

James Bond

Dr. Harold Edgerton
(1903–1990)
Institute Professor Emeritus
Professor of Electrical Measurements Emeritus
Massachusetts Institute of Technology

The legendary "Papa Flash," Dr. Edgerton was instrumental in the development of electrical circuits to create stroboscopic light, making possible high-speed photography. He adapted ultra-high-speed stroboscopic photography for night aerial reconnaissance flights during World War II and invented special marine instruments for use in his undersea work with Captain Jacques Cousteau. Two of his most famous photographs are of a crown-shaped drop of milk and of a bullet passing through an apple.

Harold Edgerton

Contents

Introduction

This book is the result of a treasure hunt we've been on for the past year and a half. But in our case, the priceless gems we sought—emeralds, rubies, sapphires, and more—could fly.

It took us eighteen grueling months to track down, photograph, and write about sixteen of the tiniest and most beautiful birds in the world. We make it a point to stress the word *grueling* because acquaintances who learned about our quest jumped to the erroneous conclusion that we were going on minivacations to fabulous resorts. The fact is that Caribbean hummers, unfortunately, are not abundant in tourist areas. They prefer, instead, some of the most remote and difficult-to-reach habitats we've ever encountered.

We allotted ourselves one visit apiece to seven islands (Puerto Rico, the Dominican Republic, Martinique, Jamaica, the Bahamas, Cuba, and Grenada) with an average stay of two to three weeks on each. Because we couldn't travel during the hurricane season (which lasts from August to October), our traveling time was limited.

How did we even know where to begin? Well, we started by contacting the eminent expert on West Indian avifauna, the late James Bond, curator emeritus of the Academy of Natural Sciences of Philadelphia. He generously provided us with a list of ornithologists and birders on each of the islands, a list that rapidly multiplied into a network of individuals anxious to assist us.

However, with the exception of Marcel Bon Saint-Côme of Martinique, none of these individuals was a specialist on hummingbirds. Instead, their expertise encompassed such diverse animals as crocodiles, bananaquits, flamingos, and lizards. Fortunately for us, they had seen the tiny birds as they conducted their studies in the field over the years and were able to recall the specific locations where they had encountered them.

But going where someone told you he last saw hundreds of hummingbirds is no guarantee that you'll see even one. Factors such as the weather, abundance of blooming flowers, and the inherent reluctance of hummers to be where you want them to be when you need them colored our success or failure on each island.

And fail we did, many times. Then there was nothing for us to do but call more people, recheck our maps, and start all over again. Sometimes we felt we were on a wild goose chase. Certainly looking for a needle in a haystack had to be easier.

Logistics at times seemed overwhelming. To begin with, our photographic work does not allow us to travel light! On each of our trips we carried ten cases containing over 400 pounds of photographic equipment, including our own gas generator for electricity. And although our island contacts had notified their customs departments of the equipment we would be bringing into each country, airport officials still panicked when they saw our luggage. In some places, such as Jamaica and the Bahamas, everything was immediately confiscated and kept in warehouses until additional government intervention could rescue them. These unexpected delays cost us valuable time.

Once our equipment had been released, we'd try to head straight out into the field. And in many instances, such as in Cabo Rojo, a tiny town in the Dominican Republic near the Haitian border, the field could only be reached after a harrowing seven-hour journey in a four-wheel-drive vehicle. City streets soon gave way to unpaved roads strewn with fallen logs and boulders, and even after encountering a roving pack of wild horses, we were finally rewarded by chancing upon a meadow of wildflowers full of Hispaniolan Emeralds.

One factor that made the birds particularly hard to find is that they do not behave much like their northern neighbors in the United States. When our American species find blooming bushes or feeders full of sugar water, they stake out territories and defend them by singing noisy, chattering songs. The wisest rule in looking for hummers in the field, then, has always been to look first for the flowers from which they feed or to listen for their distinctive songs.

The hummers in the Caribbean, however, are much less territorial. Some of them roam miles and miles back and forth throughout immense jungles feeding on a flower here, a flower there. We discovered that finding a sizable number of succulent heliconia plants, which produce one of their favorite blossoms, did not ensure the bird would stay around long enough to do more than take a perfunctory sip and then speed away, never more to be seen that day.

They are notable for their silence as well. Very few species are very vocal; the rest were just plain silent. This maddening combination of nonterritorial behavior and silence often forced us to wander from rain forest to rain forest all across an island.

Nor were weather conditions always ideal. The waves of heat and humidity were punishing, for often the cooling trade winds did not blow. Meanwhile, torrents in the rain forests stopped all activity, for hummingbirds hide when it's wet outside. Sometimes we waited days on end for the rainfall to subside only to be greeted with what seemed like thousands of mosquitos when it finally stopped.

The jungle itself was not always safe either. Fierce black ants and angry bulls left to graze by trails were difficult enough to contend with, but in Martinique we almost met our match—the deadly fer-de-lance, an extremely venomous viper found in the very jungle where we sought the Blue-headed Hummingbird. We were told that this snake, which can reach lengths of six feet or more, could be found not only slithering on the jungle floor, but also in trees and in the water. We can recall being laughed at when we attempted to show our guides how to use our snake bite kit. If you were bitten, they said, you must fall immediately to the ground, not move, and we will carry you to the hospital, where, if you do not die, you will be sick for months, the portion of your body near the bite will turn a vivid purple, and any hair on your body will turn permanently white.

Weeks later, we saw a photograph of a Jesuit priest who had survived the deadly bite. It depicted a fairly young man in a white cassock with stark white hair and beard. Even now we shiver at the memory.

In Puerto Rico, the threat took human form. Drug gangs preyed on tourists who ventured up the long winding road leading to El Yunque, a favorite local attraction and habitat of the Puerto Rican Emerald. We were constantly regaled with terrifying accounts in the newspaper and from forestry personnel telling of thieves who, not content with robbery, took satisfaction in subsequently murdering their victims. We spent one harrowing week in this area, constantly looking over our shoulders and wondering if this day would be our last.

Naturally, every precaution was taken to protect our valuable film, from special refrigerated bags, to extra supplies of Blue Ice, to arguments with airport officials who didn't want to be bothered hand-checking every item and tried to run the film through X-ray detectors.

But our share of frustration and heartbreak reached its peak when, after returning from a particularly grueling eight-week trip to Martinique and the Dominican Republic, we had the film developed only to discover that the emulsion, which had been defective, had allowed heat and humidity to ruin almost every single one of the 2,160 pictures of six hard-to-find species. There was no alternative but to make the expensive and time-consuming trip all over again.

But we happily endured film damage, drastic weather changes, physical discomfort, culture shock, and even possible bodily harm for the privilege of observing firsthand the beautiful Caribbean hummingbirds—each one unique, each one exquisite. Our admiration and love for hummers increased enormously as one by one they appeared before us.

Our most thrilling moments came when we finally located the Bee Hummingbird, the world's smallest bird, the elusive Black-billed Streamertail, and the rare Blue-headed Hummingbird, which we'd been told was almost extinct.

The rare photographs in this book represent the cream of the crop of more than 10,000 pictures taken during our trips. Both males and females are pictured, and in some cases an immature bird is represented as well. Every photograph has been carefully selected to show the bird's plumage to its best advantage in order to make identification in the field easier.

While each of the birds represented a tremendous photographic challenge, two birds, in particular, were more difficult than the rest. They are the Purple-throated Carib and the Antillean Mango, which, when seen in the air, resemble nothing more than black birds. Their iridescent plumage is extremely difficult to see with the naked eye and, thus, every possible photographic technique was used to capture these elusive colors on film.

The text is comprised of solid, informative data about each of the Caribbean species. Descriptions, locations, habitat, and nesting behavior are among the facts included to give a well-rounded portrait of each bird. In addition, an extensive study of Caribbean flora has been compiled into the most comprehensive list ever available of flowers visited and pollinated by the hummingbirds of the region.

Our journey throughout the Caribbean has now ended, but the amusing antics, sparkling feathers, and enchanting aerial powers of the world's tiniest birds will never cease to delight and mystify us.

ESTHER AND ROBERT TYRRELL

Acknowledgments

This book began with an idea that eventually became reality. But we didn't, in fact *couldn't,* have created it alone. As Americans who had never set foot on a Caribbean island, we knew we were undertaking an enormous task and that we'd never get to first base without the help of the scientists and birders who lived there.

Of the many people we wish to thank, a very special handful stand out. Their contributions both in the city and in the field were particularly essential and truly outstanding; for their efforts on our behalf we are indebted to them. They are

Marcel Bon Saint-Côme, Martinique—Antillean Crested Hummingbird, Blue-headed Hummingbird, Green-throated Carib, Purple-throated Carib;

Mrs. Audrey Downer, Jamaica—Eastern and Western Streamertails, Jamaican Mango, Vervain Hummingbird;

Dr. José Ottenwalder, Parque Zoológico Nacional, Dominican Republic—Antillean Mango, Hispaniolan Emerald, Vervain Hummingbird;

Alfonso Silva and Angel Rojas, of the Museo Felipe Poey; Francisco (Paco) Fernandez, Cinematografía Educativa (CINED); and journalist Emma Romeu, Cuba —Bee Hummingbird;

Michael Lightbourn, the Bahamas—Bahama Woodstar;

Dr. Joseph Wunderle, Jr., University of Puerto Rico/Cayey, and his wife, Dr. D. Jean Lodge, Center for Energy and Environmental Research/El Verde Field Station, Puerto Rico—Green Mango, Antillean Mango; and

George A. Vincent, Ministry of External Affairs, Agriculture, Lands, Forestry and Tourism, Grenada—Rufous-breasted Hermit, Antillean Crested Hummingbird.

Equally indispensable were David McLain, University of Maine, and Paul Sievert, University of Pennsylvania.

For their extensive help in Puerto Rico, we owe a special debt of gratitude to Wayne Arendt, USDA/Forest Service; Enrique Hernandez; and Juan Ricart, Catholic University of Puerto Rico. Also, Robert Ross, University of Puerto Rico/Cayey; Eduardo Cardona, Department of Natural Resources; Dr. Carlos Delannoy, University of Puerto Rico/Mayagüez; José Colón, Fideicomiso de Conservación; Eugenio Fernandez; Aurelio Tío, Academia Puertorriqueña de la Historia; and Ernesto Fonfrías, Instituto de Lexicografía Hispanoamericana Augusto Malaret.

Our thanks go in full measure to the following for their invaluable help in the Dominican Republic: Tomás Vargas, Departamento de Vida Silvestre, Secretaria de Estado de Agricultura; Annabelle Stockton de Dod and her husband, Donald Dod; Dr. Benjamin Paewonsky, Jardín Botánico Nacional Dr. Rafael M. Moscoso; Dr. Alfonso Ferreira, Parque Zoológico Nacional; Biol. Emilio Bautista, Departamento de Vida Silvestre, Secretaria de Estado de Agricultura; Lic. José Chez Checo, Museo Nacional de Historia y Geografía; and Lic. Bernardo Vega.

Our work in Martinique would have been much more difficult without the gracious assistance of Guy Hayot and his brother François Hayot.

In Jamaica, we were fortunate to receive the full cooperation of Catherine Levy; Anna and Clinton Black; Jean Paterson; John and Kitty Fletcher; Sir Herbert and Lady Elsie Duffus; Mrs. Alma (Lyon-Hall) Stedman; Anthony Johnson, M.P., Minister of State, Ministry of Agriculture; and Yvette Strong, Natural Resource Conservation Division, Ministry of Agriculture.

A special note of gratitude goes to the following for their kind assistance in the Bahamas: Gary Larson, Bahamas National Trust, and his wife, Susan; Michele Knowles, Department of Agriculture; Jan Harkins, Forfar Field Station/Andros Island; and Priscilla Horn, Andros Coordinator/International Field Studies/Capital University.

Nor could we have succeeded in our work on Grenada without the special assistance of Ray Walker, Forestry Service and Chasley David, South Winds Holiday Cottages and Apartments.

For assisting us in Cuba, we would like to extend special thanks to Dr. Gilberto Silva, Dr. Orlando Garrido, and Lic. Jazmín Peraza, of Museo Felipe Poey; Oreste (Chino) and Angel Martinez; Rogelio (Pelado) Garcia; Dr. Miguel Jaume; and Dr. Giraldo Alayon, Instituto de Zoología, Academia de Ciencias.

For graciously looking over data on hummingbird flowers, we wish to thank Drs. Peter Raven and Peter Hoch, Missouri Botanical Garden; Drs. W. J. Kress, D. Wasshausen, J. Wurdack, R. Read, and L. Skog, National Museum of Natural History/Smithsonian Institution; Carlos Ricart, Inter-American University (Puerto Rico); Lic. Alberto Areces, Museo Nacional de Historia Natural (Cuba); and Alain Delattre, Musée du Père Pinchon (Martinique).

With respect to the United States, we would like to give grateful acknowledgment to the late James Bond, curator emeritus, Academy of Natural Sciences of Philadelphia; Dr. Jim Wiley, U.S. Fish and Wildlife Service; Lloyd Kiff, Western Foundation of Vertebrate Zoology; Drs. Robert Colwell and Shahid Naeem, University of California at Berkeley; George Reynard; Paul Hamel, Tennessee Department of Conservation; Kimball Garrett, Los Angeles County Museum of Natural History; and Allison Andors, American Museum of Natural History.

Singular mention must go to Dr. Karl-L. Schuchmann, Zoological Research Institute and Museum Alexander Koenig, Federal Republic of Germany, not only for the tremendous help he cheerfully gave us, but also for his own outstanding work, both in the field and in the laboratory, on Caribbean hummingbirds.

Special thanks, indeed, also go to Graeme Gibson, The Great Auk, Toronto, Canada.

For generously sharing their knowledge and cheerfully obtaining hard-to-find books and journals, we wish to acknowledge the contributions of the following librarians: Katharine Donahue, History and Special Collections, UCLA, and her capable assistant, Cynthia Becht; Bea Beck, Rancho Santa Ana Botanic Garden; Almaluces Figueroa, Caribbean Regional Library, University of Puerto Rico/Río Piedras; Josefina Marxuach, Puerto Rican Collection, M.M.T. Guevara Library, University of the Sacred Heart/Santurce; and Carmen Arroyo, Centro de Estudios Avanzados de Puerto Rico y El Caribe.

For specialized work in translating foreign literature, we extend special thanks to

Herbert Kirby (German); Daniel Collins, UCLA (Russian); and Gisele Georgon, California State University at Los Angeles (French).

An added note of appreciation goes to Brent Hollister, Holly Enterprises, for keeping delicate strobes in top condition.

We are grateful to our editor, Brandt Aymar, for his dedication to our book, and wish to acknowledge our special friend, Dr. Vetura Papke, for her unfailing support and guidance every step of the way.

*Male Bee Hummingbird, the smallest
bird in the world. Playa Larga,
Cienega de Zapata, Cuba.*

Overview of the Caribbean

1

As I went along the river it was marvelous to see the forests and greenery, the very clear water, the birds, and the fine situation, and I almost did not want to leave this place. I told the men with me that, in order to make a report . . . of the things they saw, a thousand tongues would not be sufficient to tell it, nor my hand to write it, for it looks like an enchanted land.

Christopher Columbus
Tuesday, November 27, 1492

Although Columbus believed he was writing about Asia, the destination he had set out for a few months earlier, the land he actually described was that of the Caribbean. His discovery of the New World, a lush land brimming with exotic people, animals, and birds, prevails as one of the greatest achievements in history.

Before we explore the avian wonders to be found on these islands, let's first discover a few facts about the region itself.

LOCATION

The Caribbean islands, or West Indies, are a crescent-shaped archipelago extending from Florida to Venezuela. They are bounded on the west and south by the Gulf of Mexico and the Caribbean Sea, and on the north and east by the Atlantic Ocean. Approximately 2,000 miles long, the land area of the islands is 91,000 square miles, or only slightly bigger than Idaho.

There are three distinct island groupings—the Bahamas, the Greater Antilles, and the Lesser Antilles. The latter two were named by the Spanish and French in honor of the fabled Atlantic island of Antilia, or Antilla.

The Greater Antilles are Cuba, Jamaica, Hispaniola (Haiti and the Dominican Republic), and Puerto Rico. Sometimes also referred to as the Caribbees, the Lesser Antilles are the islands that lie southeast of Puerto Rico. The Lesser Antilles are further divided into the Windward and Leeward Islands. The Leeward Islands stretch from the Virgin Islands to the Saintes and the Windward Islands extend from Dominica to Grenada.

The American Ornithologists' Union, or AOU, has determined that the West Indies includes the Bahamas, Greater Antilles, the Leeward and Windward islands of the Lesser Antilles, and Swan, Providencia, and San Andres islands. Excluded are Trinidad and Tobago as well as the islands along the northern coast of South America.

We agree with these boundaries, with two exceptions. We concur with the late James Bond that San Andres and Providencia should not be included not only because their avifauna displays only a weak Antillean influence, but also because of their location on an established air route used by the migratory birds of North America.

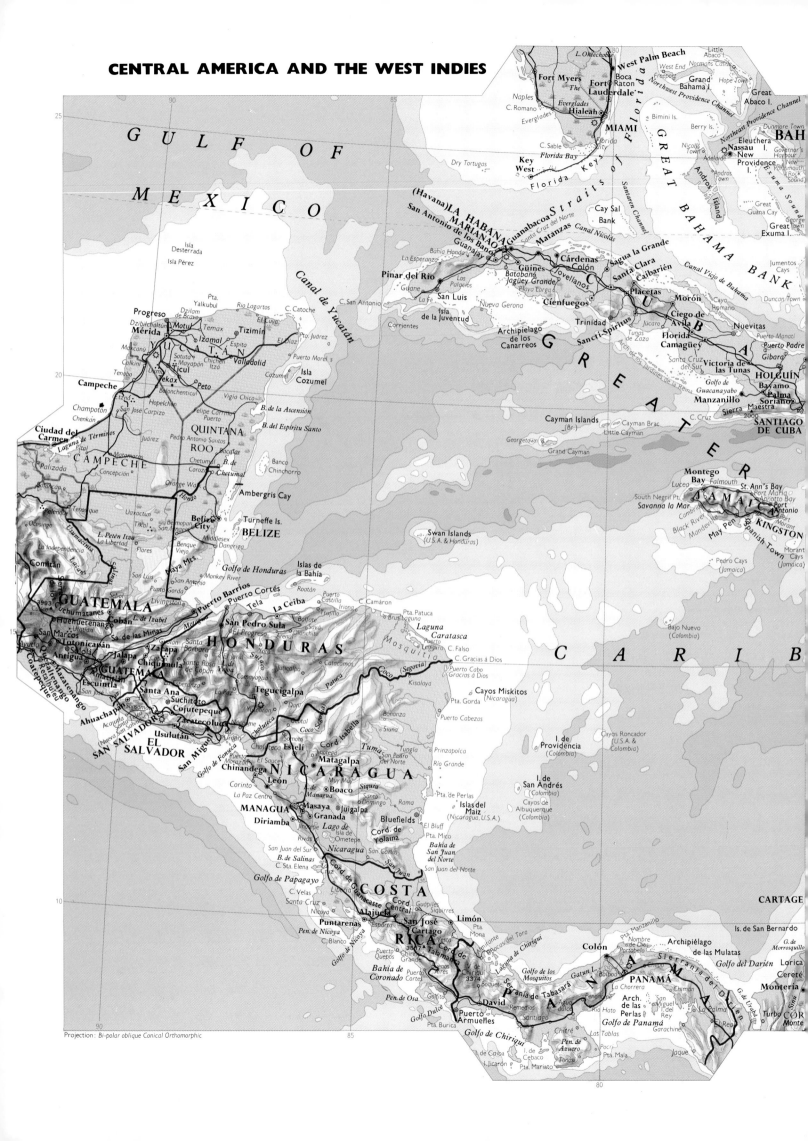

CENTRAL AMERICA AND THE WEST INDIES

GULF OF MEXICO

CARIBBEAN

Projection: Bi-polar oblique Conical Orthomorphic

1:8 000 000

Scale bars:
50   0   50   100   150   200 miles
50   0   50   100   150   200   300 km

AMAS

A T L A N T I C

O C E A N

Tropic of Cancer

Arthur's Town
The Bight
Cat I.
San Salvador
(Watling I., Guanahani)
Conception I.
Rum Cay
Long I.
Sandy Cay
Clarence Town
Crooked I. Passage
Richmond
Albert Town
Snug Corner
Acklins I.
Cay Verde
Mira por vos Cay
Plana Cays
Mayaguana I.
Cay Santo Domingo
Hogsty Reef
Little Inagua I.
Caicos Passage
Caicos Islands (Br.)
Turks Island Passage
Turks Islands (Br.)
Banes
Antilla
Mayarí
Moa
Lake Rose
Great Inagua I.
Matthew Town
Baracoa
Pta. de Maisí
Guantánamo
Î. de la Tortue
Paso de los Vientos
(Windward Passage)
Port-de-Paix
Cap-à-Foux
Cap-Haïtien
Fort-Liberté
Monte Cristi
La Isabela
Puerto Plata
Pta. Jean-Rabel
Cap-à-Foux
Golfe de la Gonâve
Gonaïves
Hinche
St.-Marc
Santiago de los Caballeros
Cordª Central
La Vega
San Francisco de Macorís
Sánchez
Sabana de La Mar
Jérémie
Î. de la Gonâve
Dame Marie
Navassa I. (U.S.A.)
Carcasse
Les Cayes
Massif de la Hotte
2280
Aquin
Î. à Vache
Jacmel
PORT-AU-PRINCE
San Juan
2280
Suriquillo
Jacmel
Pédernales
HAITI
DOMINICAN REP.
3175
Hato Mayor
San Pedro de Macorís
Higüey
La Romana
Hato Mayor
C. Engaño
B. de Yuma
Isla Saona (U.S.A.)
Baní
San Cristóbal
Azua de Compostela
Barahona
SANTO DOMINGO
Pta. de la Nagua
Nogua
L.
Î. Beata
C. Beata
HISPANIOLA
ANTILLES
Aguadilla
Arecibo
Bayamón
SAN JUAN
Virgin Gorda
Tortola
Virgin Is. (Br.)
Anegada
Sombrero (Anguilla)
Mayagüez
Isla Mona (U.S.A.)
Canal de la Mona
1338
Ponce
Caguas
Fajardo
St. Thomas
Road Town
Virgin Is. (U.S.A.)
Anguilla (Br.)
St.-Martin (Guad.)
St. Maarten (Neth.)
St.-Barthélemy (Fr.)
Barbuda
Guayama
Charlotte Amalie
Frederiksted
St. Croix
Christiansted
St. Maarten
Saba (Neth.)
St. Eustatius (Neth.)
Basseterre
ST. CHRISTOPHER-NEVIS
St. Johns
ANTIGUA & BARBUDA
Antigua
PUERTO RICO (U.S.A.)
Nevis
Redonda
Montserrat
LESSER ANTILLES
Guadeloupe Passage
Ste-Rose
Moule
Désirade
(Fr.) GUADELOUPE
Basse-Terre
Pointe-à-Pitre
Marie-Galante (Fr.)
Grand-Bourg
Î. des Saintes (Guad.)
I. de Aves (Bird I.) (Venezuela)
Dominica Passage
Portsmouth
DOMINICA
Roseau
LEEWARD ISLANDS
Martinique Passage
Ste-Marie
Mt. Pelée
1397
François
Rivière-Pilot
Fort-de-France
MARTINIQUE
St. Lucia Channel (Fr.)
Castries
ST. LUCIA
Soufrière
St. Vincent Passage
Soufrière 1234
ST. VINCENT
Speightstown
Kingstown
WINDWARD ISLANDS
Bridgetown
THE BARBADOS
Hillsborough
The Grenadines
GRENADINES
St. George's
GRENADA

B E A N   S E A
BEAN (CARIB)BEAN SEA

LESSER   ANTILLES

Aruba (Neth.)
Pta. Gallinas
Curaçao (Neth.)
Bonaire (Neth.)
Willemstad
Neth. Antilles
Is. de Aves (Ven.)
Is. Los Roques (Ven.)
I. Orchila (Ven.)
I. Blanquilla (Ven.)
I. Los Hermanos (Ven.)
Is. Los Testigos (Ven.)
Tobago
Scarborough
Pen. de la Guajira
Pta. Espada
Pen. de Paraguaná
Punto Fijo
I. La Tortuga (Ven.)
I. Margarita
La Asunción
NUEVA ESPARTA
Galera Pt.
Trinidad
C. San Román
C. San Juan de Guía
Uribia
Punta Cardón
Puerto Cumarebo
La Vela de Coro
Maiquetía
La Guaira
CARACAS
DISTRITO FEDERAL
Pen. de Paria
Río Caribe
Carúpano
Porlamar
Serpent's Mouth
Pta. Mejillones
Port of Spain
Arima
TRINIDAD & TOBAGO
San Fernando
Ríohacha
GUAJIRA
Golfo de Venezuela
Coro
FALCÓN
Tucacas
Puerto Cabello
Macuto
MIRANDA
Los Teques
Ocumare del Tuy
Río Chico
Puerto La Cruz
Cumaná
SUCRE
Caripito
Carúpano
Güiria
Golfo de Paria
BARRANQUILLA
Santa Marta
Baranoa
Cienaga
Sabanalarga
ATLANTICO
Soledad
Calamar
Fundación
MAGDALENA
San Agustín Codazzi
Villa del Rosario
Valledupar
Cuidad Ojeda
Santa Rita
La Concepción
Cabimas
MARACAIBO
Altagracia
Mene de Mauroa
Tocuyo
San Felipe
YARACUY
San Carlos
LARA
El Tocuyo
CARABOBO
Coro
Valencia
Maracay
Maiquetía
Villa de Cura
S. Juan de los Morros
Altagracia de Orituco
Aragua de Barcelona
Barcelona
Anaco
MONAGAS
Maturín
DELTA-AMACURO
Tucupita
El Tigre
Upata
Ciudad Guayana
Soledad
Sierra Imataca
El Pao
Ciudad Bolívar
Guasipati
El Callao
Tumeremo
Cutato
Mompós
Magangué
Plato
Zambrano
El Carmen de Bolívar
Sincé
Corozal
Sahagún
San Marcos
Planeta Rica
Ayapel
CUBA
BOLÍVAR
Caucasia
Simití
El Banco
Majagual
Ocaña
NORTE
SANTANDER
Cúcuta
Cordª de MÉRIDA
MÉRIDA
Ciudad Bolivia
BARINAS
Barinas
Libertad
San Fernando de Apure
APURE
San Antonio
Emb. de las Nutrias
Bruzual
Achaguas
Arauca
Apure
Orinoco
Caicara
VENEZUELA
Guanare
PORTUGUESA
Acarigua
Carora
Baragua
San Carlos del Zulia
Machiques
Lago de Maracaibo
ZULIA
CESAR
TRUJILLO
Valera
Betijoque
Trujillo
Barquisimeto
Cabudare
El Tocuyo
COJEDES
San Carlos
El Baúl
El Sombrero
GUÁRICO
Calabozo
Valle de la Pascua
Santa María de Ipire
ANZOÁTEGUI
Pariaguán
Cantaura
Unare
Tigre
Mapire
Caratal
1338
Barquisimeto
Santa Bárbara
Cordª de PERIJÁ
Catatumbo

West from Greenwich

ft   m
12,000   4000
9000   3000
6000   2000
4500   1500
3000   1000
1200   400
600   200
0   0
200   600
2000   6000
4000   12,000
6000   18,000
8000   24,000
m   ft

COPYRIGHT. GEORGE PHILIP & SON. LTD.

TOPOGRAPHY

Both the Greater and Lesser Antilles are oceanic islands. The Bahama Islands are made of coral and limestone while the Greater Antilles are the result of volcanic activity on a partially submerged continental tract. The majority of the Lesser Antilles (those islands extending from the Virgin Islands to Grenada) are also volcanic in origin, but are younger than the Greater Antilles. Barbados, Antigua, Barbuda, Anguilla, and the eastern portion of Guadeloupe are formed of coral.

Most of the islands have a mountain range in the center and some of the ridges, which have valleys between them, extend toward the sea. The highest mountain in the West Indies is the Dominican Republic's Pico Duarte, which is 10,417 feet high.

HISTORY

When Christopher Columbus landed on Samana Cay in 1492, he christened the new territory "Indies" because he erroneously believed that he had reached the East Indian islands of Asia. The name was later changed to West Indies to denote the difference.

Columbus encountered three groups of Indians when he arrived in the New World. They were the Arawaks, the Caribs, and the Guanahacabibes. Most numerous were the Arawaks, a group that was further separated into three groups: the Lucayos (Bahamas), the Tainos (Puerto Rico, eastern Cuba, and Hispaniola), and the sub Tainos (Jamaica and central Cuba). Because of their peaceful nature, the Arawaks were easily overwhelmed by both Caribs and Spaniards.

The Caribs largely inhabited the Lesser Antilles, although by 1492 they had made their way to Puerto Rico. The Guanahacabibes lived on the western end of Cuba.

Since there is no written record of these Indians, what little is known of them has come from descriptions by historians and explorers as well as studies of the few stone artifacts that have survived.

Arawaks/Tainos. Of all the native people Columbus encountered, the Tainos were by far the most culturally advanced. They were peaceful farmers whose social structure had four distinct classes, highest of which were the *caciques,* or chiefs, believed to possess mystical powers. They worshipped their ancestors, who communicated with them through shamans who functioned as both healers and priests, and revered a triangular fetish, called a zemi. Fashioned of stone, wood, or other materials, it represented spirits of animals, humans, or plants. The Tainos lived in groups as large as 3,000 people and their ceremonies were held on special dance areas and ball courts.

We know that their zemis represented the gods of nature, such as wind, earth, water, and sun. Some took the forms of birds, such as the turkey, owl, eagle, and hummingbird, and symbolized the path of the sun across the sky.

In addition, there is a direct correlation between Aztec and Taino views of the hummingbird. In both cultures the bird symbolized rebirth, since it was believed it died when the weather turned dry and was born again with the onset of the rains. Thus, it is also closely associated with the Rain God.

English words of Taino origin are *tobacco, canoe, hammock, hurricane, cassava,* and *maize.*

The Caribs. The Caribs (for whom the Caribbean Sea was named) were a warlike tribe who relied on their hunting and fishing skills for survival. Arawak was spoken by the women for only men spoke Carib and captive females were kept as slaves while their male counterparts were slaughtered and eaten.

So well known were they for this barbaric act that they were the inspiration for the

Christopher Columbus being greeted by the Indians.

Hummingbird zemi

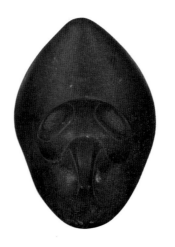

word *cannibal*. Unlike the gentle Arawaks, they were very fierce and did not submit to attempts by the Spaniards to domesticate them.

In fact, so incensed was the Spanish Crown by Carib attacks on their settlements that in 1504 it issued a royal edict decreeing that, since Christian love could not encompass cannibals, they were to be either enslaved or put to death.

Extermination of the Indians.   During the next ten years, Columbus explored and claimed for Spain nearly all of the islands in the Caribbean region. Cuba, Jamaica, and Puerto Rico were early Spanish settlements founded in the early 1500s and the new territories were ruled from Santo Domingo on the island of Hispaniola.

The Indians were enslaved and forced to work in gold mines, and by the late 1700s the combination of harsh working conditions, disease, and unspeakable cruelty at the hands of the Spanish virtually exterminated them. Those who managed to escape fled to some of the southern islands.

Perhaps the saddest consequence of the quick demise of the Indians of this area is that, of all regions on earth, the West Indies holds the singular distinction of having lost its native culture to the greatest extent.

This came about when millions of African slaves were subsequently brought in to take over the work in the sugar cane fields, an influx that led to a mixture of cultures in later generations. As a result, the vast majority of West Indians today have little or no regard for their ancestral heritage.

Meanwhile, the lure of gold and other riches attracted the attention of Dutch, English, and French pirates, who raided Caribbean ports and plundered ships along the Spanish Main.

The smaller islands were eventually colonized by the Dutch, English, French, and

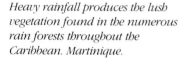

Heavy rainfall produces the lush vegetation found in the numerous rain forests throughout the Caribbean. Martinique.

Danes in the 1600s. Spain lost Jamaica to the English in 1655 and surrendered a portion of Hispaniola to the French in 1677.

Today, many of the islands in the West Indies are independent nations, while others are still linked politically with Great Britain, the Netherlands, France, or the United States.

Flora and Fauna. There is a wide variety of terrain in the Caribbean, including coastal swamps of mangrove trees that thrive on salt water and dry areas where cactus, agave, and other desert plants grow. There are also savannas and fertile lowlands, where many types of palm trees can be found. Pine forests dot the top of Hispaniolan mountains.

Where rainfall is plentiful, there are dense rain forests where tall trees of rosewood, mahogany, satinwood, and some species of ebony once grew abundantly. Unfortunately, the widespread destruction of rain forest for charcoal has resulted in the near extermination of tropical hardwoods. But epiphytes, tree ferns, lianas, orchids, heliconia, and other exotic blossoms still thrive there.

Animal life consists of reptiles, rodents, shellfish, some snakes, snails, and many varieties of insects. Birds are plentiful in the forests, although not as abundant as might be expected because of the severe hurricanes that have threatened their existence.

Hurricanes and historical disasters notwithstanding, the islands of the Caribbean continue to captivate those fortunate enough to visit them. Perhaps Columbus said it best: "... rest assured that this land is the best and most fertile and temperate and level and good that there is in the world."

Eastern Streamertail. Port Antonio, Jamaica.

Overview of Hummingbirds 2

Is it a gem, half bird, or is it a bird, half gem?

Edgar Fawcett
Birds in Natural Colors
1897

RANGE

Those of us who live in the Western Hemisphere are indeed fortunate, for only in the New World can hummingbirds be found. And although the range of this family of tiny birds stretches northward from the tip of Chile to Alaska and Labrador, there is also a rare Soviet record of a Rufous Hummingbird landing on Ratmanov Island in the Bering Strait in June of 1976.

The western boundary of their range is the Juan Fernandez group of islands in the Pacific Ocean. The eastern boundary is the island of Barbados in the Atlantic Ocean. The northernmost species is the Rufous Hummingbird and the southernmost is the Green-backed Firecrown.

Hummingbirds are tropical and subtropical, and are most abundant in the region of South America that lies between 10 degrees N and 25 degrees S. The greatest variety of species occurs in Ecuador and Colombia, and there are 163 different hummingbirds near the equator, 54 in Costa Rica, 51 in Mexico, 16 in the Caribbean, and only four in Canada.

HABITAT

Although tiny, hummingbirds are not the fragile creatures they may appear to be. Their hardiness is proven by the extreme range of climates in which they thrive. They can be found 15,000 feet up on the Andean peaks of Cotopaxi and Chimborazo, as well as in deserts, coastal swamps, and the rain forests of the Amazon.

While most species dwell in their habitat year-round, some are migratory and travel many hundreds of miles to breed in North America. One example is the Ruby-throated Hummingbird that migrates from Mexico and Central America to the eastern part of the United States. This journey sometimes includes a 500-mile-plus nonstop flight across the Gulf of Mexico. The migratory route of the Rufous Hummingbird can extend as far as 2,170 miles from southern Mexico to Alaska.

CLASSIFICATION

With respect to their place in the animal kingdom, hummingbirds belong to the order Apodiformes and the family Trochilidae.

An early attempt to classify birds was Pliny's classic *Historia naturalis,* in which he referred to wrens as *Trochilus.* In 1745, another naturalist, Barrère, concluding that

Birds display an extraordinary range of size and shape. The largest species, the Ostrich (1), towers over the man standing at its tail. Male ostriches grow to 8 feet and weigh about 300 pounds. In descending order of size are (2) the Emperor Penguin; (3) the Wandering Albatross, which has the longest wingspan of any bird at 11½ feet; (4) the Grey Heron; (5) the Peregrine Falcon; (6) Pallas's Sand Grouse; (7) the Yellow Wagtail; and (8) the Bee Hummingbird, the smallest of all species.

hummingbirds and wrens were similar, called them *both Trochilus.* A few years later, Linnaeus decided to separate these two groups again, only this time he left the hummers in the category that originally was named for the wren. Today there are 116 genera in the family, which still holds the name, Trochilidae, that hearkens back to the birds' original classification.

Linnaeus's genus was further subdivided into two genera in 1760 by the European ornithologist Brisson. The larger, curved-billed species he called *Polytmus,* while the tinier, straight-billed group was named *Mellisuga.* It was at this time, too, that French naturalists also began to differentiate hummers into two separate groups—the *Colibris* and the *Oiseaux-mouches.*

There are 339 species in the Western Hemisphere, making them the second-largest family of birds in the New World (the American Flycatcher, with 367 species, is the largest). Since 1945, thirteen new species have been discovered, leading one to believe that even more still exist!

SIZE

The tiniest hummer of all is the Bee Hummingbird, which measures slightly more than two inches in length, almost half of which is made up of its bill and tail. The largest is the Giant Hummingbird, which is a little over eight and a half inches long.

Most species are sexually dimorphic and the males can be truly dazzling with glittering feathers lavishly splashed on crowns, throats, and breasts. Sometimes they also have fabulous trains and crests. Females, who solely rear the young, are often camouflaged by their gray and brown plumage, while some, like the Anna's and Costa's, have small sparkling patches on their throats. Happily, there are exceptions, and both males and females of some species, like the Violet-crowned Hummingbird, Buff-bellied Hummingbird, and Green Mango are equally dazzling.

As a rule, those hummers with glittering feathers live in sunny habitats that allow their beauty to be shown to best advantage.

NAMES

The sparkling plumage of hummingbirds has prompted many to resort to a jeweler's vocabulary to describe them. Indeed, some of their names, such as the Gilded Sapphire, Ruby-topaz, and Glittering Emerald directly allude to polished gems. There are also groups known collectively as the Emeralds, Brilliants, Sapphires, Mountain-gems,

One member of the glittering Emerald family is the Cuban Emerald. Andros Island, Bahamas.

Starthroats, and Firecrowns. In fact, they are so often compared to jewels that in zoos throughout the world aviaries housing them are always known as "jewel rooms."

Some hummers have fanciful names that have nothing to do with jewels, but everything to do with the charm with which they obviously captivated those who first saw them. These are the diminutive Coquettes, Sunangels, Hillstars, Comets, Plumeleteers, Fairies, Sunbeams, and Woodstars.

There are some species, however, that do not possess the beautiful garb of their glittering cousins. Because they live primarily in the dark interior of tropical forests, they do not need feathers that sparkle in the sun. Instead, their feathers are primarily brown and gray, and because of their drab attire they are known as "hermits."

The Taino word for hummingbird, *colibri,* means "god bird," or "sun god bird." Today, this word is still used by the Italian, Portuguese, and French to mean hummingbird. The Dutch call it *kolibrie* or *kolibrielje,* while the Germans say *kolibri.* The Tainos also called it *cacique,* which meant chieftain.

The different local names given to hummingbirds by West Indians are almost as varied as the islands themselves. They allude to the characteristic humming noise produced by the bird's fast wingbeat, its tiny size, the picturesque way it feeds from blossoms, and its glittering feathers.

In Spanish, *zumbar* means "to buzz or hum," so it comes as no surprise to hear Puerto Ricans and Dominicans calling the bird *zumbador.* Cubans also attempted to imitate the whirring wings by referring to it as *zunzún.*

In Martinique, the rapid wingbeat reminded the French-speaking inhabitants of the swishing sound made by women's skirts as they brushed against a dance floor. This noise, called a *frou-frou,* was later shortened to *fou-fou.*

Many names, like the French *oiseau-mouche ("fly bird")* and the Spanish *paxaro mosquito* ("mosquito bird") clearly compared the bird to small insects. And the Spanish also called it *tominejo,* a name derived from the small unit of measure known as a *tomin* and a word once used to denote anything tiny, as well as *cominejo,* an allusion to the tiny grains of the spice cumin.

If you've ever seen a hummer sipping nectar from a flower, you'll be able to understand those who chose to give it a name that reflected its dainty feeding habits. These names include *chupaflor,* which literally means "flower sucker" (South America), *chuparosa,* or "rose sucker" (Mexico), and *beija flor,* or "flower kisser" (Brazil).

In the French West Indies, the Purple-throated Carib was christened *madère* in all probability because the warm tints of its throat bring to mind those of a good Madeira wine. They also called it *bourdoneur* and *murmures.* Likewise, ancient Mexicans used words like *huitzitzil, pigada,* and *ourbiri* to liken the bird's beautiful feathers to "rays of the sun" and "tresses of the day star." And in northern South America, the hummingbird is called *limpiacasa,* or "housecleaner," because it is often seen along ceilings and dusty corners hunting for spiders and insects to eat.

Ouanga négresse, the Haitian name for the hummer, recalls a ritual of black magic in which the bird was once used as a love potion.

PHYSICAL CHARACTERISTICS

Hummingbirds are the smallest birds in the world and are easily identified by their long, needlelike bills. Their closest relatives are the swifts and, like them, have four pairs of ribs, legs that are short and weak, and pointed claws.

They also have the greatest flight capability of any bird since they are capable of flying not only forward, but also backward, to the right and to the left, hovering, and even flying upside down. No other birds have wings that beat faster, and with respect to smaller birds, they fly the fastest.

Relatively speaking, the hummingbird has the fastest metabolic rate of any warm-blooded animal, the largest heart of all warm-blooded animals, and one of the largest brains of any bird.

The drab plumage of some hummingbirds, like that of this Rufous-breasted Hermit, has earned them the name "hermits." Grand Étang, Grenada.

The resemblance between the deep red hues of the Purple-throated Carib and those of a fine Madeira wine probably account for its French name of "Madère." Lamentin, Martinique.

And, if you've ever watched them at length, you have probably noticed that they are curious, quarrelsome, and intolerant of other birds or animals that may enter their territories.

LONGEVITY

How long do hummingbirds live? Well, although there are records of English aviculturists keeping hummers in captivity over eight years and banded Brazilian hummingbirds living to nine, their life expectancy can exceed ten years. The New York Zoological Park has records for both a Green-throated Carib and a Purple-throated Carib surviving over ten and a half years and there are Blue-throated and Broad-tailed Hummingbirds that have reached the age of twelve.

PREDATORS

Because hummingbirds have always been prized for their shimmering plumage, one of their greatest predators over the centuries has been man. Fortunes were made by brokers who obtained skins from individuals in South America and the West Indies and then sold them to the European and American markets. There designers and milliners dressed fashionable ladies with bonnets, hats, fans, and other accessories trimmed with the sparkling feathers of the unfortunate birds.

As a rule, hummingbirds were downed with rifles filled with small shot, or even blowpipes. But in Martinique, a new way was found to capture these elusive birds.

Using a glue made from the milk of a certain West Indian tree, young boys would glue flowers to a long branch. They would then hold the branch up to a flowering

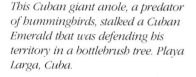
This Cuban giant anole, a predator of hummingbirds, stalked a Cuban Emerald that was defending his territory in a bottlebrush tree. Playa Larga, Cuba.

tree until all the blossoms blended in. Hummingbirds feeding on the flowers would soon become accustomed to the branches and, when close enough, would unwittingly get stuck. The children would then wrap the bodies in leaves, dry them in the fire, and trade them when bartering with French sailors for hooks and pins. Why would sailors want dried hummingbirds? Their girlfriends had discovered that they made lovely drop earrings.

Natural enemies of adult hummingbirds include hawks, orioles, frogs, bass, and insects like the praying mantis.

Nor do helpless nestlings fare well, particularly in tropical regions. One female Bahama Woodstar that had made its nest in a bunch of bananas returned to find that a rat had eaten both the chicks and the bananas. In another instance, a person who had been observing the growth of two nestlings noticed a whipsnake coiled near the now-empty nest. He killed it on the spot and found the two babies inside. Incredibly, one was still alive! It was returned to its nest where it continued to thrive and eventually fledge.

In Jamaica, a Golden Silk, or Brushfooted Spider, spun its web next to the nest of a Vervain Hummingbird. This particular spider is an orb weaver whose webs, measuring six and a half feet to almost ten feet in length, are the biggest in the world. Its silk is so strong that it is sometimes used to make cloth.

It should come as no surprise, then, that the tiny mother was soon caught in the web. Luckily, she was spotted by two men working nearby who freed her. A few days later, the men again noticed the female in the web, but this time they were too late. The little bird had evidently been killed by the spider, since close inspection revealed two punctures on one side of her neck. The spider was immediately killed. The Vervain's eggs did not survive.

As if this weren't danger enough, there are also large lizards who prey on unsuspecting hummingbirds. The Cuban giant anole, or chipojo, lies in wait among the foliage of flowering trees and ambushes the hummer as it unsuspectingly sips from blossoms.

This reptile, which can reach a length of over five and a half inches, eats not only small and large hummingbirds, small warblers, and frogs, but also smaller lizards. It is endemic to Playa Larga, a region in the Peninsula of Zapata. *Anolis baracoae,* which reaches a length of over six and a half inches, is another species that often eats hummingbirds.

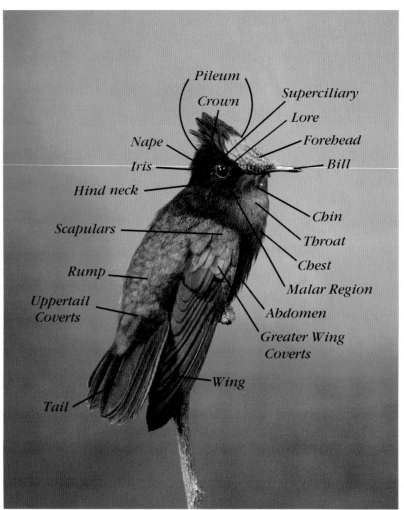

Pileum
Crown
Superciliary
Lore
Nape
Forehead
Iris
Bill
Hind neck
Chin
Scapulars
Throat
Chest
Rump
Malar Region
Uppertail Coverts
Abdomen
Greater Wing Coverts
Wing
Tail

The parts of a bird. Antillean Crested Hummingbird. St. George's, Grenada.

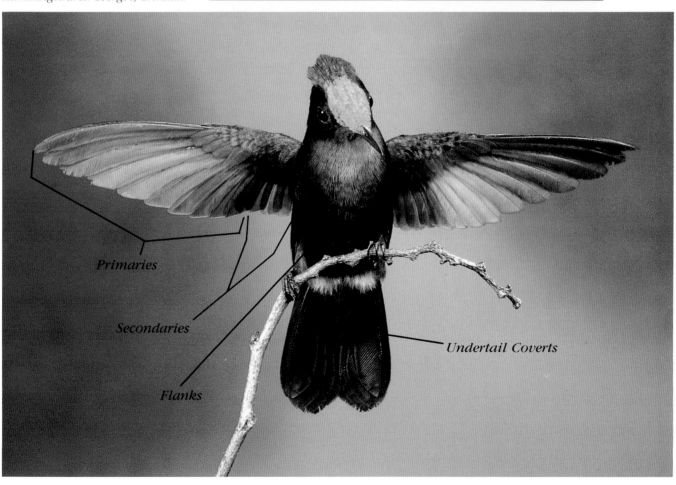

Primaries
Secondaries
Flanks
Undertail Coverts

A Portfolio of Caribbean Hummingbirds

3

So have all Ages conceaved, and most are still ready to sweare, the Wren is the least of Birds, yet the discoveries of America . . . shewed us one farre lesse, that is the Hum-bird, not much exceeding a Beetle.

Thomas Morton
The New England Canaan
1632

The first Europeans to see hummingbirds were those who came to the New World with Columbus. The naturalists and explorers that followed him were fascinated with the bird and sent back word of a tiny creature that seemed to have the characteristics of a bird, an insect, and a butterfly.

The hummingbirds of the Caribbean belong to nine different genera, five of which are endemic, or native, to the region. These endemic genera are *Cyanophaia, Eulampis, Mellisuga, Orthorhyncus,* and *Trochilus.* Fifteen of the sixteen species found there are endemic to the West Indies: the Bee Hummingbird, Cuban Emerald, Puerto Rican Emerald, Green Mango, Green-throated Carib, Antillean Crested Hummingbird, Vervain Hummingbird, Western Streamertail, Eastern Streamertail, Jamaican Mango, Blue-headed Hummingbird, Hispaniolan Emerald, Antillean Mango, Purple-throated Carib, and the Bahama Woodstar. The only exception is the Rufous-breasted Hermit whose range is South America, including Trinidad and Tobago, as well as southern Central America.

The eight species endemic to the particular islands on which they are found are the Bee Hummingbird (Cuba), Puerto Rican Emerald (Puerto Rico), Green Mango (Puerto Rico), Bahama Woodstar (the Bahamas), Eastern and Western Streamertails (Jamaica), Jamaican Mango (Jamaica), and the Hispaniolan Emerald (Hispaniola).

The Ruby-throated Hummingbird, a migrant to the West Indies, has been recorded in Cuba, Hispaniola, and the Bahamas. Although there are sightings for Jamaica and Puerto Rico, they have not been substantiated.

AFFINITIES OF WEST INDIAN HUMMINGBIRDS

The Antilles were long considered part of the Neotropical or South American region, but analyses of the avifauna by the late James Bond show their affinity to that of North America. The majority of birds are similar to, or reminiscent of, those of the eastern United States, but not of Mexico.

The South American element in the Antilles comprises parrots and parakeets, a potoo, hummingbirds (probably), and tyrant flycatchers. Among these there are endemic genera only of hummingbirds. The ancestors of all other endemic genera (thirty-four) were of northern origin.

Greater Antillean and Bahaman genera of Trochilidae were derived from North America, apart from the Lesser Antillean *Orthorhyncus* and *Eulampis holosericeus.*

Western Streamertail. Kingston, Jamaica.

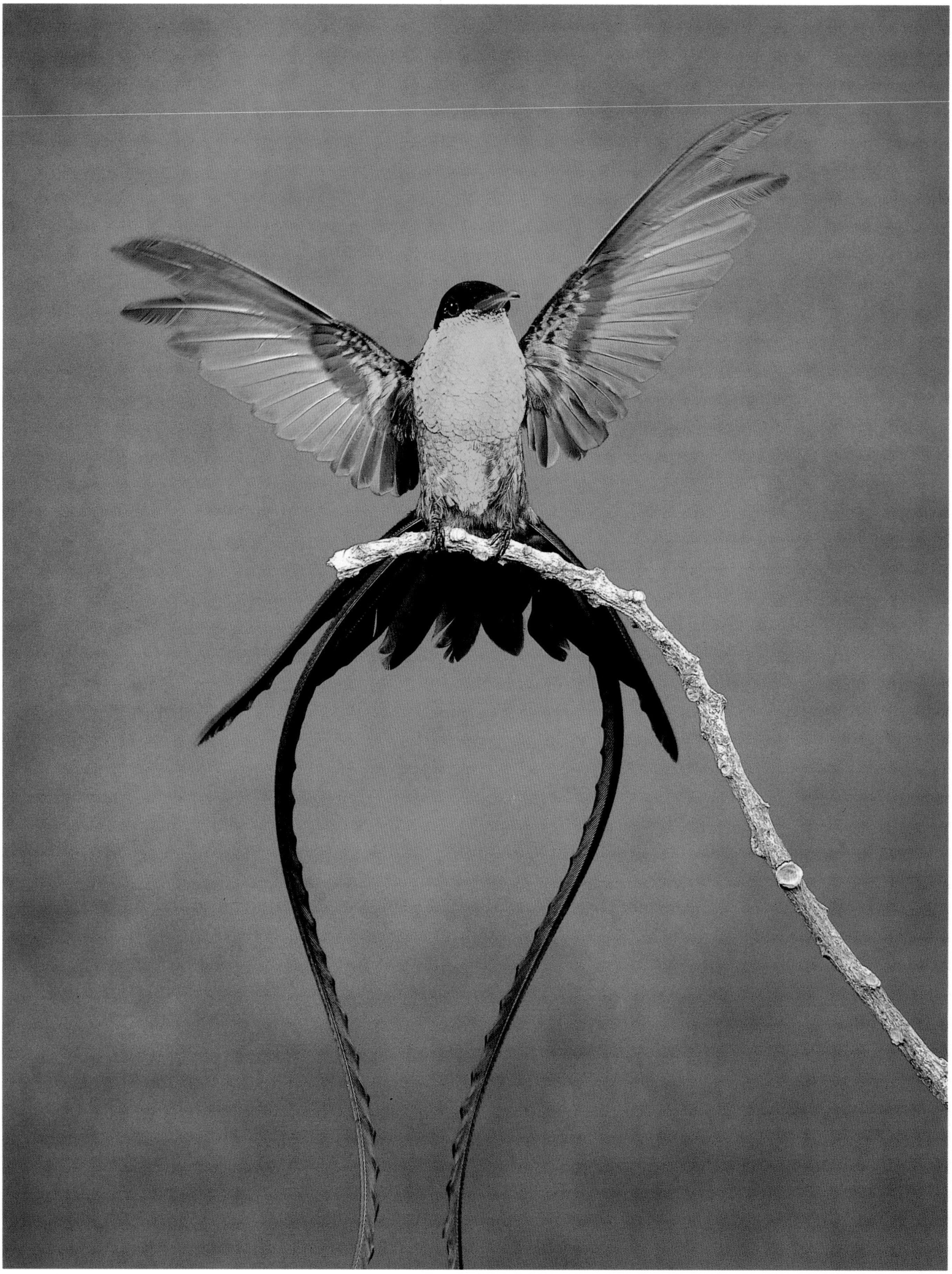

The endemic genera are *Trochilus* and *Mellisuga* of the Greater Antilles, and *Cyanophaia* of the Lesser Antilles. *Orthorhyncus* and *Eulampis* are two genera endemic to both the Greater and Lesser Antilles and are believed to be derived from extinct South American genera.

No fossilized remains of hummingbirds have been found in the Caribbean, yet it has been determined that the oldest hummingbirds on the Lesser Antilles are *Orthorhyncus* and *Eulampis,* and the fact that there are two forms of *Trochilus* on Jamaica indicates that this genus has been there a long time as well.

Distinct similarities to other genera in the hummingbird family have been determined for those of the West Indies. For example, *Mellisuga* is related to *Calypte* and *Archilochus,* both North American species, while *Cyanophaia* appears to be allied to the *Cynanthus,* which is found in Mexico and the southwest U.S. *Orthorhyncus* is close to *Chrysolampis* of South America.

The ancestors of *Chlorostilbon, Calliphlox,* and *Anthracothorax* reached the Greater Antilles from Central America (southern North America). *Glaucis* is a recent arrival in Grenada from Trinidad or Tobago; it is not even subspecifically distinct from the nominate South American race.

Why is it that the hummingbirds of North America are not as diverse as those from South America? Well, it has been suggested that at one time there *did* exist numerous additional species of hummingbirds in this specific area, but the fact that they were so specialized made it easier for them to be wiped out during the Ice Age, which affected food sources such as certain essential types of flowers.

Fortunately for us, the species of the Caribbean are among the loveliest of all hummingbirds. Their graceful beauty has been captured in the portfolio that follows.

THOSE FLYING "DOCTOR BIRDS"

*"Docta bud a cunny bud,
Hard bud fe dead."
("The doctor bird is a
cunning bird,
A hard bird to kill.")*

Frederic Cassidy
Jamaica Talk
1961

On many islands of the Caribbean, particularly Jamaica, where it is the national bird, the hummingbird is known as the "Doctor Bird." While no one knows for certain the exact origin of this nickname, there are many theories as to how the bird came to be associated with doctors.

For example, since West Indian druggists at one time were also the local taxidermists, it was assumed that hummingbird skins sold to them were used to make medicines.

Some Jamaicans believe that the crest and elongated tail feathers of the Streamertail Hummingbird are reminiscent of the top hats and long-tailed coats once worn by physicians. Others see a distinct similarity between the bird's long bill and a surgical lancet. Also, when Jamaican country people see hummingbirds piercing the base of flowers to get to the nectar source within, they say that the birds "medicine" the plants, thus again calling to mind the image of a doctor.

However, we believe the answer lies with the Arawaks, one of the earliest tribes to inhabit the Caribbean region. They believed that the hummingbird brought tobacco to their ancient ancestors, no doubt because they had seen it feeding from its blossoms and nesting among its branches. Since the fragrant plant was their first, or most important, medicine, native healers relied upon its curative powers, and for this reason the hummingbird came to be associated with early medicine men, or "doctors," and earned the name "Doctor's Bird."

While there are no longer Arawaks in the Caribbean, those that inhabit parts of South America refer to the hummers in their own regions as the "doctor bird" to this day.

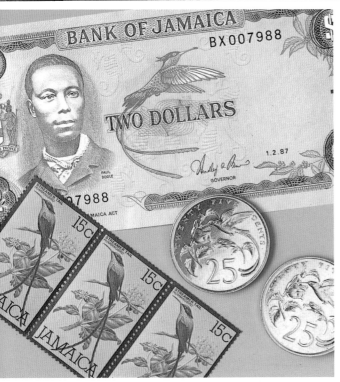

Because the Western Streamertail is the national bird of Jamaica, it is depicted on both currency and coins.

Hummingbirds are known throughout the Caribbean as "doctor birds."

Male Antillean Crested Hummingbird (Orthorhyncus cristatus). *Lamentin, Martinique.*

Antillean Crested Hummingbird

No bird is more pugnacious than this tiny mite; he will attack birds twenty times his own size, especially Hawks, and even a male and female cannot meet without a slight difference of opinion. I have noticed the little hummers busily engaged around the flowers, when suddenly they have heard the sound of a fight, and they have gone off in the direction like the shot from a gun. Like the proverbial Irishman, if there is a row he will be there. . . .

Sydney Porter
"Notes on the Birds of Dominica"
Avicultural Magazine
1930

GENUS	*Orthorhyncus*
SPECIES	*Orthorhyncus cristatus*

ORIGIN OF SCIENTIFIC NAME	*orthorhyncus:*
	    ortho (Greek)—straight
	    rhyncus (Greek)—bill
	cristatus (Latin)—crested

LOCAL NAMES	In Puerto Rico: Crested Hummingbird, Doctor Bird, Little Doctor Bird, Zumbador, Zumbador Crestado, Zumbadorcito, Zumbadorcito Crestado
	In Montserrat: Sparrow
	In the French West Indies: Coulibri, Colibri Huppé, Fou-Fou, Frou-Frou Huppé, Oiseau-Mouche Huppé
	In Barbados: Doctor Booby
RANGE	Resident on Puerto Rico, Culebra, Vieques, Virgin Islands, and the Lesser Antilles, including Antigua, Montserrat, Îles des Saintes, Dominica, Martinique, St. Lucia, St. Vincent, Barbados, Barbuda, Bequia Island, Union Island, the Grenadines, and Grenada.
	One specimen collected in Galveston Island, Texas, in 1967.
	Puerto Rico—Fajardo to Ceiba
	Antigua—Including Great Bird Island and Long Island, Wallings Reservoir
	Montserrat—Jubilee Heights, Garibaldi Hill, Chance's Summit
	Dominica—Plaisance
	Martinique—From sea level to the top of Mt. Pelée, Fort-de-France, Caravelle Peninsula; also often seen flying at sea between Martinique and St. Lucia or between Martinique and Dominica
	St. Lucia—Edmund Forest Reserve, Cas-en-bas, Quilesse
	St. Vincent—Cumberland Valley, Will-Be-Free
	Barbuda—Trail to Darby Cave
	Grenada—Annandale Falls, Concord Falls, Grande Anse, Point Salines, Morne Delice, Grand Étang, Mt. Granby, Belvedere, Mt. St. Catherine

Female Antillean Crested Hummingbird (Orthorhyncus cristatus). *Lamentin, Martinique.*

HABITAT   Gardens and other cultivated areas as well as understory of forests at various elevations.

DESCRIPTION   **Adult male**

Iris:	dark brown
Bill:	straight; dull black
Crest:	brilliant metallic green turning into bright blue-green at the tip
Forehead and crown:	bright metallic green
Loral and ear regions and underparts:	sooty black
Chin and throat:	dark gray
Hind neck and sides of head:	dull metallic blue-green
Upperparts:	dull metallic green
Wings:	dusky, glossed with purple
Tail:	slightly rounded; black, glossed with purple-bronze
Feet:	dusky

Adult female

Iris:	similar to male
Bill:	similar to male
Crest:	less conspicuous than that of the male
Chin and throat:	dull white
Upperparts:	metallic green
Underparts:	light gray; slightly darker on the sides
Wings:	dusky, glossed with purple
Tail:	more strongly rounded than that of the male
middle pair:	metallic green with gray-brown tips
remaining pairs:	black, glossed with purple
three outer pairs:	black, glossed with purple; wide gray tips
Feet:	dusky

Male Antillean Crested Hummingbird. Note its molting primaries and tail.

When agitated or angry, the bird raises its crest to signify its displeasure.

Immature male	Similar to adult male except
Crest:	none
Pileum:	dull metallic blue-green

MEASUREMENTS	**Male**		**Female**	
Length:	3.1–3.75 in.	Length:	2.9–3.1 in.
Wing:	1.8–1.9 in.	Wing:	1.8 in.
Tail:	1.1 in.	Tail:	0.9–1.1 in.
Bill:	0.4–0.6 in.	Bill:	0.4–0.6 in.

WEIGHTS **Male** 2.2–4.3 g

Female 2.0–3.4 g

VOICE The distinctive "pit-chew" of a gunshot combined with other varied harsh notes. Distress call is "tchick-tchick."

COURTSHIP The female sits about 20 inches away from the male, who, with his brilliant green crest erect, hovers in front of her. Wings whirring, he flies slowly toward her before producing a sharp noise by hitting his wings against his tail feathers. He then dazzles her with the brilliant iridescence of his crest, which changes color as he rapidly flies four to six times in an arc in front of her, each time punctuating the flight with the sharp mechanical tone created by his feathers. They then mate.

The courtship display of the Antillean Crested Hummingbird.

NESTING Breeds year-round. The female can build her nest in five days and usually situates it from 2 to 7 feet from the ground in a variety of trees such as the nutmeg, citron, tamarind, and pomegranate as well as vines and shrubs.

Composed of cobwebs, flecks of bark, tiny dried leaves, and fern scales, the nest is often lined with silky plant fibers, like those of the corkwood tree, that are so white that the nestlings, which are born with long, red downy feathers, are easily noticed. The little mother lays two white eggs that measure about 11.6 mm x 8 mm. Incubation takes about fifteen days and the babies will remain in the nest twenty-one days before fledging.

This series of photographs shows how the female Antillean Crested Hummingbird fluffs out her feathers before landing on her nest.

The nests of the Antillean Crested Hummingbird vary from island to island. The first three are from Martinique, and the rest are from St. Vincent and Grenada.

29

The female Antillean Crested Hummingbird that constructed this nest subsequently abandoned it, but returned later to pilfer its material for use in building her new one.

The female who built this nest constructed it on an artificial flower. She came back later to rebuild a new nest on top of the old one. Lamentin, Martinique.

Male Antillean Crested
Hummingbird/Parrot's Plantain
(Heliconia psittacorum).

Female Antillean Crested Hummingbird/Red Ginger (Alpinia *aff.* purpurea). *Grand Étang, Grenada.*

ANTILLEAN CRESTED HUMMINGBIRD

The unscreened windows of many Caribbean homes and buildings allow the female Antillean Crested Hummingbird to be unusually creative in her choice of nesting sites. One, for example, raised several broods in a nest built on the rope upon which a chandelier was suspended. Another chose a wire that supported a light fixture in the middle of a classroom of Jesuit seminarians, where, in spite of the distractions of both noisy students and the booming voice of the professor, she raised not one, but two nestfuls of chicks.

The tiny mother sometimes experiments with different building materials, too. For example, one, who was building a nest in a vase of artificial flowers in a dining room, swooped down on the residents as they were eating dinner and tried to pull hairs from the father's head. Elsewhere a gentleman was surprised when a tiny hummer attempted to pluck strands from his eyebrows!

We found a charming nest built in a wicker lamp hanging from a ceiling and spent hours watching her zoom in and out a nearby window to a garden outside, where she nourished herself from an abundance of tropical blooms.

Male Antillean Mango
(Anthracothorax dominicus).
Jarabacoa, Dominican Republic.

Antillean Mango

The bird was alert and active on the wing, whirling, poising and shifting its position with the greatest celerity. The long tail was nervously expanded and gyrated from side to side . . . as the bird whirled from flower to flower. The sun was reflected from its plumage as it passed through rays of light with a strong sheen of copper.

Alexander Wetmore and Bradshaw Swales
The Birds of Haiti and the Dominican Republic
1931

GENUS *Anthracothorax*

SPECIES *Anthracothorax dominicus*

ORIGIN OF SCIENTIFIC NAME *anthracothorax:*
    anthraco (Greek)—coal
    thorax (Greek)—chest

dominicus (Latin): Refers to Santo Domingo, capital of the Dominican Republic, one of the two countries making up the island of Hispaniola.

LOCAL NAMES In Puerto Rico: Doctor Bird, Hummingbird, Puerto Rican Golden Hummingbird, Colibrí Dorado, Zumbador, Zumbador Dorado, Zumbaflor, Zun-zún, Zunzún Dorado

In the Dominican Republic: Zumbador Grande

In Haiti: Ouanga Négresse

RANGE Resident on Hispaniola (Haiti and the Dominican Republic), Gonâve, Tortue and Beata Islands and Île-à-Vache; Puerto Rico, Mona Island, and, possibly, St. Thomas.

Haiti—Port-au-Prince, Morne la Visite, Terrier Rouge, Morne des Mammelles, La Hotte, Desbarriere, Camp Perrin, Jacmel, Belladère, Las Cahobes, Pétionville, Étang Saumâtre, Petit-Goâve, Jérémie, Trou des Roseaux, Moline, Rivière Bar, Bombardopolis, Fort Liberté, Montfleury, Damien, L'Arcahaie, Étang Miragoane, Fonds-des-Nègres, L'Acul, La Tremblay, Kenskoff, Hinche, Caracol, Cap Haïten, Gonaïves

Gonâve Island—En Café

Dominican Republic—Santo Domingo, Jarabacoa, Barahona, Habanero, Puerto Plata, Samaná, La Vega, Cabo Rojo, Caña Honda, El Valle, Río San Juan, Sánchez, Monte Cristi, Sosúa, Chocó, Laguna, Rojo Cabo, Constanza, Azua, Haina, Sabana San Thomé, San Juan de la Maguana, Laguna del Salodillo, Aquin

Puerto Rico—Quebradillas, Manatí, Bayamón, Martin Peña, Mameyes, Humacao, Patillas, Maunabo, Salinas, Juana Diaz, Yauco, Guánica, Cabo Rojo, Aguadilla, Lares, Comerio, Ciales, Aibonito, Añasco, Hucares, Arroyo, Cataño, Boquerón, Maricao, Cayey, Carite Forest, Guánica State Forest, El Tuque, Ponce, coastline from Salinas to Toa Baja

Mona Island—Playa de Pájaros

Female Antillean Mango
(Anthracothorax dominicus). *Cayey,
Puerto Rico.*

HABITAT	Common in open clearings, gardens, and scrubby hillsides in both moist and semidry areas. Although numerous along the coast, some can also be found in lightly wooded mountainous regions.

DESCRIPTION **Adult male**

Iris:	brown
Bill:	decurved; black
Chin and throat:	metallic green-bronze
Upperparts:	metallic green-bronze
Underparts:	velvety black on chest, fading into dull brown-gray on sides, flanks, and lower abdomen
Wings:	dusky, faintly glossed with violet
Tail:	slightly rounded or emarginate
middle pair:	bronze with blue-black tips
remaining pairs:	dark violet-chestnut glossed with violet and with blue-black tips
Under tail coverts:	dusky
Feet:	dusky

Adult female

Iris:	similar to male
Bill:	similar to male
Chin and throat:	gray-white passing into paler white on abdomen
Upperparts:	metallic bronze-green
Sides and flanks:	sometimes mixed with metallic bronze
Wings:	dusky, glossed with violet
Tail:	slightly rounded or emarginate
middle pair:	bronze-green
remaining pairs:	violet-brown at the base with steel-blue stripe and white tips
Under tail coverts:	gray
Feet:	dusky

Immature male Antillean Mango (Anthracothorax dominicus). San Cristóbal, Dominican Republic.

Immature female Antillean Mango
(Anthracothorax dominicus). *Cayey,*
Puerto Rico.

Immature male Antillean Mango
preening his wing feathers.

Immature male	Similar to adult female except
Throat and chest:	black median line
Tail:	
Outer pairs:	chestnut at the base and glossed with violet

MEASUREMENTS	*Total length:* 4.5–5 in.
Male	
Wing:	2.2–2.4 in.
Tail:	1.3–1.7 in.
Bill:	0.9 in.

Female	
Wing:	2.3–2.4 in.
Tail:	1.4–1.5 in.
Bill:	0.8–0.9 in.

| **WEIGHTS** **Male** | 5.6–8.2 g |

| **Female** | 4.0–7.0 g |

| VOICE | Loud, discordant chirping and harsh staccato notes |

| COURTSHIP | Data not available. |

| NESTING | The breeding season for this bird extends from March to August. Nests are built from 7 to 33 feet from the ground and may be placed in wild almond trees or even the stem of the banana plant. The outside of the nest is bound with flecks of bark and cobwebs, while the inside is composed of soft plant down. It is approximately 40 mm in diameter and 32 mm high and each of the two white eggs measures about 15.5 mm × 10 mm. |

The nest of the Antillean Mango. Western Foundation of Vertebrate Zoology

The nest of the Antillean Mango. Jarabacoa, Dominican Republic.

Female Antillean Mango/Sanchezia
nobilis. *Cayey, Puerto Rico.*

Male Antillean Mango/Coral Plant (Russelia equisetiformis). *Note the protruding feather—the result of a recent fight with another hummingbird. Santo Domingo, Dominican Republic.*

Male Bahama Woodstar (Calliphlox evelynae). *Nassau, Bahamas.*

Bahama Woodstar

They are both curious and pugnacious... and while walking through the woods one of these birds would often alight close by or hover over our heads, as if examining us....

John I. Northrop
"The Birds of Andros Island, Bahamas"
Auk
1891

GENUS	*Calliphlox*
SPECIES	*Calliphlox evelynae*

ORIGIN OF SCIENTIFIC NAME	*calliphlox:*
	    calli (Greek)—beautiful
	    phlox (Greek)—flame
	evelynae: French naturalist Jules Bourcier gave the bird its name, possibly to honor his wife.

LOCAL NAMES	God Bird, Hummingbird
RANGE	Resident on the Bahama Islands; possibly northern Cuban cays; casual in southern Florida (Miami, Lantana, and Homestead). The Bahama Islands—New Providence Island, Great Inagua Island, Little Inagua Island, San Salvador, Andros Island, Grand Bahama Island, Great Abaco Island, Grand Turk, Great Ragged Island.
HABITAT	Mixed pine forests, coastal brushlands, open clearings and gardens.

DESCRIPTION **Adult male**

Iris:	dark brown
Bill:	straight (or very slightly decurved); dull black
Head:	there is a white spot behind the eye
Chin and throat:	metallic red-purple that deepens into violet as it extends downward
Chest:	white that deepens into gray-brown
Upperparts:	dull metallic green, duller on crown
Rest of underparts:	rufous with paler central portion
Sides and flanks:	glossed with metallic bronze-green
Wings:	dusky and faintly glossed with purple
Tail:	deeply forked
middle pair:	dull metallic green
outermost pair:	purple-black
second pair:	dull metallic green tinged with purple-black and with part of the outer web cinnamon
third and fourth pairs:	pale rufous
Under tail coverts:	rufous that turns into buff or white on the sides
Feet:	dusky

Female Bahama Woodstar (Calliphlox evelynae). *Nassau, Bahamas.* Note: *Back view shows bird feeding from hibiscus* (Hibiscus rosa-sinensis).

Adult female

Iris:	dark brown
Bill:	straight (or very slightly decurved); dull black
Forehead:	gray-brown
Chin and throat:	dull white
Upperparts:	dull metallic green
Chest:	gray-white
Underparts:	rufous with paler central portion
Tail:	double rounded or rounded
three outer pairs:	very pale rufous at the base with wide band of purple-black and broad green or cinnamon tips
Under tail coverts:	light rufous
Feet:	dusky
Immature male	Similar to adult female
Immature female	Similar to adult female except
Upperparts:	rufous color mixed in with the green

Immature male Bahama Woodstar (Calliphlox evelynae). *Nassau, Bahamas.*

MEASUREMENTS	*Total length:*	3.5–3.75 in.
Wing (female):	1.5–1.75 in.	
Tail (male):	1.1–1.4 in.	
Bill:	0.7 in.	
WEIGHTS	**Male**	2.7–2.8 g
	Female	2.7–2.9 g
VOICE	Basic note is a rapid "tit, titit, tit, tit, titit." Song is "prititidee, prititidee, prititidee."	

COURTSHIP   The display was beautifully described in 1891 by naturalist
John Northrop:

> *The female was perched on a branch of a low shrub
> and before her the male was performing. His wings were
> vibrating rapidly in the usual manner, and thus
> supported in the air he swung rapidly to and fro, at the
> same time rising and falling, a movement very difficult
> to describe but almost exactly like that of a ball
> suspended by an elastic thread that stretches and
> contracts as the ball swings back and forth. This
> exceedingly graceful movement was executed through a
> small arc for a few minutes, and then was suddenly
> changed.*
>
> *The male expanded his tail, showing the cinnamon of
> the webs, and then threw himself rapidly and almost
> violently from side to side in an almost horizontal line.
> During this latter part of the display a rustling sound
> was produced, probably by the vibrations of the wings,
> and a few short sharp notes were uttered.*

*A female Bahama Woodstar built her
nest in this plant* (Hoya carnosa). *A
little green lizard used to sunbathe
on one of the leaves and one day he
was so startled by the little mother
that he accidentally leaped onto her
nest! When the hummingbird saw the
lizard sitting near her eggs, she
pecked him on his head as she
buzzed back and forth in front of
him until he finally jumped to the
ground. The female bird then went
back to incubating her eggs, turning
her body until she was well settled.*

He then darted suddenly at the female who all the while had been sitting apparently unconcerned, seemed almost to touch her with his bill, and then flew rapidly away. Shortly afterward the female left, flying in another direction. During all of the display the two birds were facing each other and not more than six or eight inches apart, and the gorget and tail of the male were exposed to their fullest advantage.

Our own observations during a January trip to Nassau concerned a male that was chasing a female around and around a 15-square-foot area. They were often face to face during a good part of this chase, which took place considerably low to the ground and lasted about a minute. She finally flew to a nearby bush and hung nearly upside down, her exhaustion preventing her from sitting upright. The male positioned himself 4 to 5 inches from her and proceeded to move back and forth in a smooth arc for about 30 seconds, during which time he kept his beak open and made harsh, chattering sounds. Another quick chase followed, this one leading them to a lemon tree where, from a distance of only 3 inches from the female, he made a series of 12-inch arcs, each of which stopped abruptly in the center. He did this for a minute.

NESTING   The nest, a compact egg cup composed of soft plant down and decorated with bits of bark, is usually built at a distance between 3 and 13 feet from the ground. Like other hummingbirds, the female probably lays two eggs at a time, although nests containing one and even three eggs have been discovered. The eggs, which are white with a pinkish cast and measure about 12 mm × 8 mm, take at least fifteen days to incubate. Although the female generally nests during April, this species may breed anytime throughout the year.

The nest of the Bahama Woodstar. Nassau, Bahamas.

Male Bahama Woodstar/Cape Honeysuckle (Tecomaria capensis)

Male Bahama Woodstar/Hibiscus (Hibiscus rosa-sinensis). *Note the extensile use of the tongue.*

Male Bahama Woodstar/Coral Plant
(Russelia equisetiformis)

Female Bahama Woodstar/Cape Honeysuckle (Tecomaria capensis)

Male Bee Hummingbird (Mellisuga helenae). *Playa Larga, Ciénega de Zapata, Cuba.*

Bee Hummingbird

Bill half an inch. Tail half an inch. Head and body three quarters of an inch. One could hardly believe it to be a bird, and how this minute creature lasted out through severe ocean storms . . . to Germany, puzzles one.

H.D.A.
"(Notes) Humming Birds"
Avicultural Magazine
1914

Note: This is the smallest bird in the world and was recently put on the endangered species list.

GENUS *Mellisuga*

SPECIES *Mellisuga helenae*

ORIGIN OF SCIENTIFIC NAME
mellisuga:
  melli (Latin)—honey
  suga (Latin)—suck

helenae: Named in honor of Helena Booth, benefactress of Juan Gundlach, the Cuban naturalist who first identified the bird.

LOCAL NAMES Zunzuncito, Sunsuncito, Zumbete, Sumbete, Zumbador, Zumbadorcito, Pájaro Mosca, Pájaro Mosca Cubano, Trovador, Colibrí

RANGE Resident on Cuba and Isla de la Juventud.

Cuba—Cárdenas, Santiago, Bayate, Figuabas, Los Gallegos, Playa Larga, Guantánamo, Cojíma, Hacienda Jiquí on Cochinos Bay, Maria la Gorda, Guanahacabibes Peninsula, Santo Tomás, Ciénega de Zapata, Holguín, Maniadero, Los Ávalos, Pálpite, Soplillar, Ojito de Agua, Cruzata, Jaguaní River, Cayo Probado, Farallones, Moa, Las Cuevas

HABITAT Gardens, swampland, forests, and shrubbery, although sometimes seen in more open areas.

DESCRIPTION **Adult male**
  Iris: dark brown
  Bill: straight; dull black
  Head: iridescent fiery red
  Sides of throat: elongated feathers extend outward
  Hind neck to upper tail coverts: metallic blue-green
  Underparts: dull white on chest, deepening to deep gray on abdomen
  Sides and flanks: metallic blue-green, mixed with gray
  Wings: dusky, faintly glossed with violet
  Tail: emarginate; metallic blue
  side pairs: metallic blue with wide black tips
  Under tail coverts: gray with a darker tip
  Feet: dusky
  Adult female
  Iris: similar to male
  Bill: similar to male
  Pileum: dull metallic green, deepening to blue toward the back

Female Bee Hummingbird (Mellisuga helenae). *Santo Tomás, Ciénega de Zapata, Cuba.*

VOICE   The vocalizations of the male Bee Hummingbird are made up of a shrill metallic song and a lower-pitched buzz that can be uttered in many different combinations. It often makes a piercing twitter while it perches.

COURTSHIP   The male perches on a high branch and proceeds to sing a lengthy song. The female, meanwhile, has taken her place on a very low branch near the ground. The male makes two u-shaped arcs in the air in front of the female after which copulation takes place.

NESTING   Breeding takes place in May and June. The female builds her nest 8 feet from the ground. The nest, which measures 30.5 mm in diameter and 12.8 mm in depth, is relatively large, considering the bird's tiny dimensions. Loosely woven, it is made of dried vegetable fibers and has a soft inner layer of plant wool. The female lays two white eggs, each about 11.4 mm × 8.2 mm in size.

Sound spectrogram of the vocalization of the Bee Hummingbird. (A) song; (B) buzz; (C) twitter.

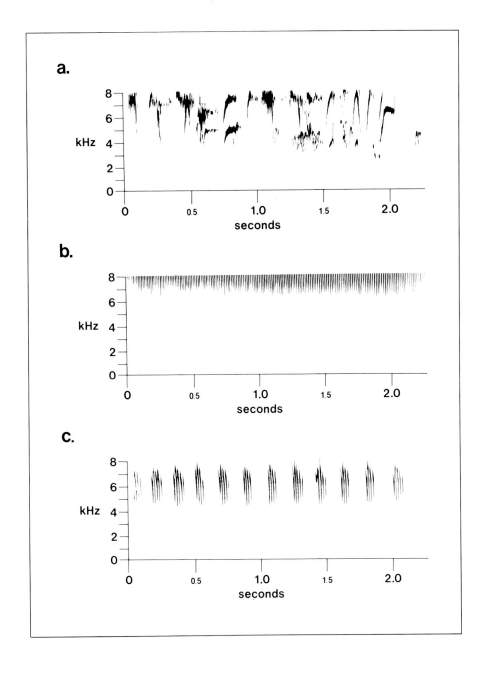

Superciliary, ear, and eye regions:	brown-gray, with a black streak in front of the eye and a white spot behind it
Upperparts:	metallic green with blue tints
Underparts:	pale brown-gray, fading into white in lower areas
Wings:	dusky, faintly glossed with violet
Tail:	rounded
middle pair:	bright metallic blue-green
two outermost pairs:	bright blue-green at the base with wide black bands and tipped with white
remaining pairs:	bright green-blue at the base, tipped with black
Under tail coverts:	dull white
Feet:	dusky

Immature male	Similar to adult female except
Upperparts:	usually more blue

MEASUREMENTS **Male** **Female**

	Male		Female
Length:	2.17–2.18 in.	*Length:*	2.41 in.
Wing:	1.16 in.	*Wing:*	1.25–1.4 in.
Tail:	0.66 in.	*Tail:*	0.52 in.
Bill:	0.39 in.	*Bill:*	0.48 in.

WEIGHTS	**Male**	1.95 g
	Female	2.6 g

Male Bee Hummingbird landing on a penny.

Female Bee Hummingbird stretches leisurely.

The nuptial dive of the Bee Hummingbird.

The nest of the Bee Hummingbird. Santo Tomás, Ciénega de Zapata, Cuba.

Male Bee Hummingbird/Flame of the Woods (Ixora coccinea)

*Female Bee Hummingbird/*Duranta erecta

58

Male Bee Hummingbird/Coral Plant
(Russelia equisetiformis). *Each*
tubular blossom measures
approximately 1 inch in length.

Female Bee Hummingbird/Coral Plant (Russelia equisetiformis)

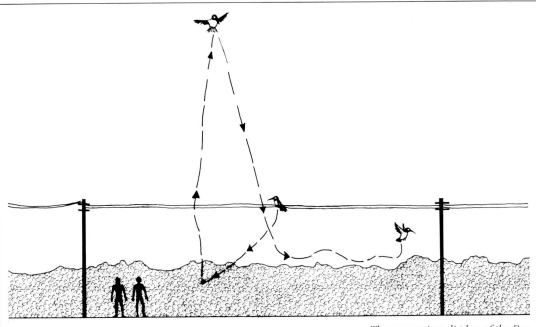

The aggression display of the Bee Hummingbird

The Bee Hummingbird, like some other species, is territorial. When an unwanted guest ventures into its flowery domain, it will perform a show of aerial acrobatics designed to frighten away the intruder.

Around noon on a sunny day in Los Ávalos, Cuba, two members of our team were the targets of an aggressive display by an angry male who had been keeping watch from his perch on a telephone wire.

It flew downward toward them and stopped suddenly for 2 to 4 seconds. It then zoomed up to a great height only to stop again briefly for 1 to 2 seconds. A final downward dash at a higher speed ended when the bird flew in the opposite direction toward the dense foliage. This dive was repeated three times in a row.

A member of our team films the habitat of the male Bee Hummingbird. The bird's favorite perching spots were the tops of the highest trees as well as telephone wires.

Inset *Below the trees was an abundant supply of the Scarlet Bush* (Hamelia patens), *a favorite nectar source. Los Ávalos, Ciénega de Zapata, Cuba.*

Male Blue-headed Hummingbird
(Cyanophaia bicolor). *Lamentin,*
Martinique.

Blue-headed Hummingbird

It is a fair-sized Humming-bird, the under parts being jet black and the upper parts the well known Humming-bird green, but the whole of the wing coverts are an amazingly brilliant emerald green which flashes and glistens in the sunlight.

Sydney Porter
"Notes on the Birds of Dominica"
Avicultural Magazine
1930

GENUS	*Cyanophaia*
SPECIES	*Cyanophaia bicolor*

ORIGIN OF SCIENTIFIC NAME	*cyanophaia:*
	    cyano (Greek)—dark blue
	    phaia (Greek)—shine
	bicolor (Latin)—two-colored

LOCAL NAMES	Colibri
	Male: Frou-Frou Bleu, Colibri Tête-Bleu
	Female: Fou-Fou Feuille Blanc, Colibri Falle-blanc
RANGE	Resident on Dominica, Martinique, St. Vincent, and other islands of the Lesser Antilles.
	Dominica—Syndicate, Plaisance
	Martinique—Chemin Bouliqui at the foot of the Pitons du Carbet, Colson, La Medaille, Les Deux Choux, Fort-de-France, above the village of Belle Fontaine at Verrier, the slopes of Mt. Pelée and the Pitons du Carbet, frequent near the highway crossing the rain forest between Fort-de-France and Morne Rouge.
	St. Vincent—Layou
HABITAT	Common in open areas and undisturbed forests at high elevations from 1,600 to 4,000 feet; seldom seen at sea level.

DESCRIPTION **Adult male**

Iris:	dark brown
Bill:	straight; upper portion is black and lower portion is pink at base and black at tip
Head, chin, and upper throat:	metallic violet-blue
Lower throat and chest:	bright metallic blue-green
Hind neck to upper rump:	bronze-green
Lower rump, shorter upper tail coverts:	blue-green
Longer upper tail coverts:	dark green-blue
Underparts:	bronze-green
Wings:	glossy blue-black
Tail:	emarginate; dark blue
Feet:	dusky

Adult female

Iris:	similar to male
Bill:	straight, dusky

Female Blue-headed Hummingbird
(Cyanophaia bicolor). *Lamentin,
Martinique.*

Pileum:	metallic green
Malar region:	gray-brown
Underparts:	pale gray-brown
Sides and flanks:	gold-green
Hind neck to rump and upper tail coverts:	gold-green
Wings:	dusky glossed with violet
Tail:	emarginate
two middle pairs:	metallic bronze deepening into blue-green near the tips
third and fourth pairs:	dark green-blue; metallic bronze at the base; tipped with pale brown-gray
outermost pair:	similar to fourth but pale gray tip still broader

Immature male Blue-headed Hummingbird

A preening female Blue-headed Hummingbird

MEASUREMENTS

	Adult male		Adult female		Juvenile male	
Total length:	3.9 in.	*Total length:*	3.7–3.8 in.	*Total length:*	3.8 in.
Bill:	0.8 in.	*Bill:*	0.7–0.8 in.	*Bill:*	0.8 in.

WEIGHTS

Adult male   4.5–4.7 g   **Adult female**   3.9–4.7 g   **Juvenile male**   4.2 g

VOICE   A series of shrill metallic notes, rapidly descending in pitch. The distress cry is a metallic "click-click-click."

Nest of the Blue-headed Hummingbird. Martinique

Nest of the Blue-headed Hummingbird Western Foundation of Vertebrate Zoology

COURTSHIP   Data not available.

NESTING   This bird, which breeds from March to May, builds its nest about 8 feet from the ground. If the nest is situated in a fern, the female may use some of its filaments, combined with palm fibers, in the construction. Bound to the branch by spiderwebs, the nest may also contain roots and twigs and be decorated with small strips from the heliconia plant. Fluff from the silk-cotton tree may line the cup, but sometimes there is no soft interior at all. The nest measures 58 mm in height and 47 mm in diameter and is considerably deep compared to those of the other Antillean species. The two white eggs measure about 13.5 mm × 8.6 mm.

The habitat of the Blue-headed Hummingbird. The bird sometimes feeds from the bushes of the Wild Strawberry, which grows along the road. Martinique

The tropical rain forest where we found the Blue-headed Hummingbird. This is also the habitat of the deadly fer-de-lance snake. Martinique

Male Blue-headed Hummingbird/
Bananier d'Ornement (Musa ornata)

*Male Blue-headed Hummingbird/
Pendant Firebirds* (Heliconia
rostrata)

Male Cuban Emerald (Chlorostilbon ricordii). *Andros Island, Bahamas.*

Cuban Emerald

. . . This little "Hummer" darts . . . [about] looking like an emerald dragon fly, whirring and hovering close to one with complete fearlessness, and the next moment away across the room to sip honey from flowers in a vase.

Hubert D. Astley
"Powers of Resuscitation in Humming Birds"
Avicultural Magazine
1914

GENUS	*Chlorostilbon*
SPECIES	*Chlorostilbon ricordii*

ORIGIN OF SCIENTIFIC NAME	*chlorostilbon:*
	    chloro (Greek)—green
	    stilbon (Greek)—glitter

	ricordii: Named for Philippe Ricord, the French surgeon and naturalist, who first introduced the bird to Europe.
LOCAL NAMES	In the Bahamas: Hummingbird, Emerald Hummingbird, God Bird
	In Cuba: Colibrí, Picaflor, Trovador, Visitaflor, Zumbador, Zumbete, Zunzún
RANGE	Resident on Cuba, Isla de la Juventud, Cayo Coco, Cayo Largo, and other nearby cays, and the Bahamian islands of Grand Bahama, Green Cay, and Andros. Casual in remaining areas of the Bahamas. Vagrant to southern Florida.
	The Bahamas—Grand Bahama, Green Cay, Andros, Great Abaco
	Cuba—Havana, Santiago de Cuba, Figuabas, Palmarito, Pinár del Rio, Monte Verde, El Guamá, Cabañas, Trinidád, Holguín, San Diego de los Baños, Batabano, Matanzas, San Cristóbal, Bemba, Soledad, Playa Larga, Ojo de Agua del Roble, Los Gallegos, road to Salinas, Oriente, Playa Giron, Santo Tomás, Ciénega de Zapata, Soplillar
	Isla de la Juventud—Almacigos, Santa Fé
HABITAT	Thickets, forests, parks, and gardens.
DESCRIPTION	**Adult male**
Iris:	dark brown
Bill:	straight; upper portion is dull black and lower portion is pinkish
Crown:	dull bronze-green
Eye area:	white spot behind the eye
Upperparts:	dark metallic bronze-green
Underparts:	bright metallic green
Wings:	dusky, glossed with violet
Tail:	deeply forked
two outer pairs:	green-black or black, faintly glossed with blue-green
third pair:	similar but with green-black inner webs
two middle pairs:	dark green-bronze
Under tail coverts:	white, sometimes streaked with gray on the sides
Feet:	dusky

Female Cuban Emerald
(Chlorostilbon ricordii). *Andros Island, Bahamas.*

Adult female

Iris:	similar to male
Bill:	similar to male
Crown:	brown-gray
Eye area:	similar to male
Upperparts:	dark metallic bronze-green
Underparts:	gray-brown
Sides (from neck to flanks):	metallic green
Tail:	deeply forked
Feet:	dusky

MEASUREMENTS *Length:*

Male	3.6–4.0 in.
Female	3.8 in.
Wing:	1.9–2.2 in.

Tail:

Male	1.75 in.
Female	1.5 in.
Bill:	0.7 in.

WEIGHTS   **Male**   2.9–4.6 g   **Female**   2.9–4.1 g

VOICE   Double-noted call of metallic "tic-tics," sometimes repeated three times, but, more often, four times in a row.

COURTSHIP   Data not available.

Cuban Emerald nestlings. Baby hummingbirds gape when their sensitive downy feathers are ruffled by the wings of the mother. For this photograph, Robert gently blew on their backs and they responded.

Nests of the Cuban Emerald. Santo Tomás, Ciénega de Zapata, Cuba.

NESTING   This nest is more loosely woven than those of other
           Caribbean species and is composed of moss and silky
           vegetable fibers. Some are held together with long trailing
           tendrils of bark and their exteriors are often flecked with
           bark and lichens.

           Often found close to the ground, they can be built in the
           forks of young branches of coffee bushes as well as on
           vines that hang from trees like the paw-paw. Like some
           other hummingbird species, this bird sometimes builds her
           new nests directly on top of her old ones.

           The clutch consists of two eggs, approximately 13 mm × 9
           mm in length, and nestlings have dusky-colored
           uppperparts and pale underparts. Their stubby bills are
           also dark above and lighter below.

           The female, who breeds throughout the year, is particularly
           fearless, and if a large bird, such as a buzzard, gets too
           close to her nest, she has no qualms about chasing it away.

           When the nest of one female was destroyed in a hurricane,
           she built a new one in a chandelier located in the study of
           Juan Gundlach, one of Cuba's most renowned
           ornithologists! In that safe little spot, she proceeded to raise
           four separate nestfuls of chicks, rebuilding the original nest
           each time.

*This Cuban Emerald nest from
Andros Island, Bahamas, was
particularly well camouflaged by the
fern fronds that surrounded it.*

Male and female Cuban Emeralds/
Barleria cristata. *Andros Island,*
Bahamas.

76

Blossoms from Tabebuia rosae *are a favorite of the Cuban Emerald. Playa Larga, Ciénega de Zapata, Cuba.*

Green Mango (Anthracothorax viridis). *Sexes are alike. El Yunque, Puerto Rico.*

Green Mango

These birds were active, pugnacious and alert, and pursued one another or other hummers about flowering plants or through the aisles of the forest with dash and vigor, the light reflecting from their brilliantly metallic plumage as they flew rapidly about.

Alexander Wetmore
Scientific Survey of Porto Rico and the Virgin Islands
1927

GENUS	*Anthracothorax*
SPECIES	*Anthracothorax viridis*

ORIGIN OF SCIENTIFIC NAME	*anthracothorax:*
	    anthraco (Greek)—coal
	    thorax (Greek)—chest
	viridis (Latin)—green

LOCAL NAMES	Colibrí Verde, Puerto Rico Mango, Zumbador Verde, Zumbador Verde de Puerto Rico, Zunzún Verde, Zunzún Verde de Puerto Rico
RANGE	Resident on Puerto Rico. Puerto Rico—El Yunque, Adjuntas, Utuado, Lares, Mayagüez, Mameyes, Río Piedras, Caguas, Maricao Forest, Aibonito, Cayey, El Verde, Toro Negro, Carite and Caribbean National Forest, Bosque Susua Forest, Ponce, Luquillo Mountains
HABITAT	Common in dense forests, forest edges, and coffee plantations, particularly those of the mountainous areas of the interior; sometimes seen on the coast.

DESCRIPTION	**Sexes alike**	
	Iris:	dark brown
	Bill:	decurved; black
	Pileum:	dull green
	Upperparts:	metallic green
	Underparts:	metallic blue-green
	Wings:	dusky, glossed with violet
	Tail:	rounded or emarginate; metallic blue-black
	outer feathers:	sometimes tipped with gray
	Feet:	dusky
	Young	Similar to adult except
	Underparts:	darker and duller or narrowly tipped with gray-brown

MEASUREMENTS	*Total length:*	4.5 in.
	Wing:	2.3–2.6 in.
	Tail:	1.4 in.
	Bill:	0.9–1.0 in.

WEIGHTS	6.6–7.2 g	
VOICE	The song is a series of quiet chirps while the call is a shrill one-note cry.	

COURTSHIP   Data not available.

NESTING   Nests are built from December to February, although some have been observed as early as October. There is a great similarity between the nest and eggs of this bird and those of the Antillean Mango Hummingbird in that both build small round cups made of soft plant fibers embellished with chips of lichen into which two tiny white eggs are laid. The plumage of the male fledgling is like that of the adult.

Male Green Mango in molt. Note the new protruding tail feathers.

Male Green Mango getting ready to clean its bill. Hummingbirds use their claws to scrape away pollen and other foreign materials.

Male Green-throated Carib (Eulampis holosericeus). *Lamentin, Martinique.*

Green-throated Carib

In the very heart of the great tropical forests . . . where subdued green twilight always reigned, we found this little gem. . . . I saw it long after the twilight had fallen when I could hardly tell whether it was a beetle or a bird.

Sydney Porter
"Notes on the Birds of Dominica"
Avicultural Magazine
1930

Note: Also called the Emerald-throated Hummingbird, this bird is sometimes placed in the genus *Sericotes*.

GENUS	*Eulampis*
SPECIES	*Eulampis holosericeus*

ORIGIN OF SCIENTIFIC NAME	*eulampis:*
	    eu (Greek)—beautiful
	    lampis (Greek)—torch, lamp
	
	holosericeus:
	    holo (Greek)—wholly
	    sericeus (Latin)—silken

LOCAL NAMES	Doctor Bird, Green Doctor Bird In Puerto Rico: Blue-breasted Hummingbird, Emerald-throated Hummingbird, Green Carib, Zumbador, Zumbador de Pecho Azul, Zumbador Pechiazul In the French West Indies: Colibri, Colibri Falle-Vert, Colibri Vert, Doctor Carcoo, Fou-Fou, Fou-Fou Tête Longue
RANGE	Resident on Puerto Rico (eastern and, rarely, western portion), Vieques, Culebra, Culebrita, the Virgin Islands, and Lesser Antilles, including St. Martin, Saba, St. Eustatius, Antigua, Barbuda, Dominica, Martinique, St. Lucia, St. Vincent, Barbados, Bequia, and Union Islands. Puerto Rico—Fajardo and Ceiba, Rincón, Manatí, Vega Baja Antigua—Sugar Loaf Mountain, Body Ponds, Maid Island, Shirley Heights, Wallings Reservoir Barbuda—Trail to Darby Cave Martinique—Throughout the island, Fort-de-France, Route de Moutte, Crève Coeur, the Peninsula of Caravelle. Sometimes seen flying between the main island and the very small islets one mile away. St. Vincent—Brighton, Kingstown Botanic Garden, Camden Valley, Buccament Valley Grenada—Grand Étang, Mt. Granby, Belvedere, Mt. St. Catherine, Concord Falls, Annandale Falls
HABITAT	Gardens, cultivated areas and rain forests at all elevations. Seems to prefer dry terrain in Martinique.

Female Green-throated Carib (Eulampis holosericeus). *Sexes are similar except for the longer, more decurved bill of the female. Also, the blue portion of the abdomen is narrower in the female. Lamentin, Martinique.*

DESCRIPTION	Sexes are similar except the bills of females are longer and more decurved than those of the male.
Adult	
Iris:	dark brown
Bill:	decurved (that of the female is longer and more decurved than that of the male); black
Malar region, chin, and throat:	metallic green
Upperparts:	metallic green deepening to blue-green on upper tail coverts
Chest:	
center:	violet-blue patch
sides:	blue-green
Underparts:	black, glossed with green and blue
Wings:	dusky with faint violet gloss
inner secondaries:	glossed with green
Tail:	rounded; blue-black
Under tail coverts:	metallic blue
Feet:	dusky
Immature	Similar to adult except
Chin, throat, and chest:	dull metallic green
Underparts:	duller
MEASUREMENTS *Total length:*	4.1–4.75 in.
Wing:	2.25–2.5 in.
Tail:	1.3 in.
Bill:	0.8–1.1 in.

WEIGHTS **Adult male** 5.6–7.8 g **Adult female** 4.9–5.5 g

Juvenile male 5.5–5.6 g **Juvenile female** 4.3–5.1 g

The exquisite iridescence of the throat and breast of the Green-throated Carib is virtually impossible to see when the bird is in flight.

VOICE   This bird makes a harsh "chewp" that is accompanied by a noisy rustling of the wings.

NESTING   Although it may breed year-round, this bird generally nests from late March to mid-July. It is believed to enter a period of nonsexual activity after the dry season, at which time it molts. Low sites are usually chosen for the nest, although some have been observed at distances of 7 to 30 feet from the ground. Nests are well camouflaged by the foliage of tropical vegetation and can be very difficult to find.

Similar to that of the Antillean Mango Hummingbird, the nest is composed of leaves and bark. Soft downy filaments from certain cacti may be used for the lining and the two white eggs measure approximately 15.1 mm × 9.3 mm.

In Martinique, a special 6-foot-high, 12-foot-square scaffolding was constructed in order to not disturb a nesting Green-throated Carib as she was photographed. Her movements were observed through a tiny crack in the platform.

The soft interior of the nest of the Green-throated Hummingbird is cottony fibers.

A Green-throated Hummingbird incubates her eggs.

The nest of the Green-throated Hummingbird

*The beautiful Flamboyant tree, found
on nearly every Caribbean island, is
truly a hummingbird "restaurant."
Many different species could be
observed feeding from it throughout
the day.*

Male Green-throated Carib/Torch
Ginger (Etlingera elatior)

Male Hispaniolan Emerald
(Chlorostilbon swainsonii). Note:
Back view shows bird feeding from
Wild Plantain (Heliconia bihai). *Las*
Mercedes, Dominican Republic.

Hispaniolan Emerald

*It was common in the damp, deciduous rain forests, keeping principally in the shade,
anywhere from ground level to the tops of the trees. In early morning when the air was
damp it came out occasionally to feed in the open growths of pine. The wings produce
a loud humming in flight.*

Alexander Wetmore and Bradshaw Swales
The Birds of Haiti and the Dominican Republic
1931

GENUS   *Chlorostilbon*

SPECIES   *Chlorostilbon swainsonii*

ORIGIN OF SCIENTIFIC NAME   *chlorostilbon:*
     chloro (Greek)—green
     stilbon (Greek)—glitter

swainsonii: Named for the English naturalist William Swainson.

LOCAL NAMES   In the Dominican Republic: Zumbador, Zumbador Verde, Zumbaflor

In Haiti: Colibri, Ouanga Négresse, Wanga Neges Mon

RANGE   Resident on Hispaniola (Dominican Republic and Haiti) and, possibly, Gonâve Island.

Dominican Republic—La Sierra de Neiba, Las Mercedes, Sierra de Baoruco, Cachón de la Rubia, Hato Mayor, Bonao, Jarabacoa, Constanza, Quita Espuela, Sánchez, El Río, Catarry, Aguacate, La Vega, Samaná, El Valle, La Canita, Loma Tina, Loma Pelona, Loma Rucilla, San Cristóbal

Haiti—Citadelle Hill, Morne Trechant, Geffrard, Les Glaces, Desbarriere, La Cour Z'Anglais, Pic de Macaya, Massif de la Selle, Massif de la Hotte, Bombardopolis, Kenskoff, Gantier, Pétionville (Le Coup), Mont Rouis, head of the Rivière Chotard

HABITAT   Although particularly numerous in thick vegetation and shady portions of rain forests, it can also be found in open clearings.

DESCRIPTION   **Adult male**
     Iris: dark brown
     Bill: straight; upper portion is dull black and lower portion is pinkish with dusky tip
     Crown: dull bronze-green
     Chin, throat, sides of chest: metallic emerald-green
     Center of chest, upper breast, and abdomen: velvety black
     Rest of underparts: metallic green, darker along the median line
     Upperparts: metallic bronze-green
     Upper tail coverts: more bronzy than upperparts
     Wings: dusky, faintly glossed with purple
     Tail: deeply forked; dark green-bronze
     outer pairs: dull black
     Feet: dusky

Female Hispaniolan Emerald
(Chlorostilbon swainsonii). *Las*
Mercedes, Dominican Republic.

Adult female	Similar to male except
Underparts:	pale brown-gray
Sides and flanks:	washed with metallic green
Tail:	
side pairs:	bronze, with black tips
one or two outermost pairs:	bronze, with black stripe; tipped with brown-gray

MEASUREMENTS	*Total length:*	4.0 in.
	Wing:	1.9–2.25 in.
	Tail (**male**):	1.75 in.
	Tail (**female**):	1.5 in.
	Bill:	0.7 in.

WEIGHTS **Male** 4.4–5.0 g **Female** 2.5–4.6 g

Nest of the Hispaniolan Emerald
Western Foundation of Vertebrate
Zoology

*After a grueling eight-hour journey
in a four-wheel-drive vehicle, we
finally chanced upon a meadow
of* Rhytidophyllum auriculatum
*blossoms that were being visited by
Hispaniolan Emeralds. Las Mercedes,
Dominican Republic.*

VOICE	A series of metallic, staccato "tics."
COURTSHIP	Data not available.
NESTING	The nest, which is considerably large for a hummingbird of this size, is built 3 to 6 feet from the ground. Its bottom is made of moss and fern fibers, while bits of both soft and coarse plant filaments make up the interior. The exterior is composed of cobwebs speckled with lichens. It measures 50 mm in diameter, 60 mm to 65 mm in height, and the interior of the cup is 20 mm in depth.

Male Hispaniolan Emerald/Barbados Pride (Caesalpinia pulcherima)

Male Hispaniolan Emerald/Aechmea *sp.*

Male Jamaican Mango
(Anthracothorax mango). *Crystal Spring, Jamaica.*

Jamaican Mango

Its tail is its chief beauty. . . . This fine tail is continually flirted widely open as the bird is feeding, and makes a beautiful purple fan. . . . To see a sight like this is worth braving all the terrors of the Atlantic.

George E. Lodge
"Notes on Some of the West-Indian Humming-birds"
Ibis
1896

GENUS	*Anthracothorax*
SPECIES	*Anthracothorax mango*
ORIGIN OF SCIENTIFIC NAME	*anthracothorax:*
	anthraco (Greek)—coal
	thorax (Greek)—chest
	mango (Latin): polished gem or stone
LOCAL NAMES	Doctor Bird, Hummingbird
RANGE	Resident on Jamaica.
	Jamaica—Kingston, Hope Gardens, Port Antonio, Port Henderson, Spanish Town, Priestman's River, Moneague, Morant Point, Cockpit Country, John Crow Mountains, Crystal Springs, Hardwar Gap, Montego Bay
HABITAT	Can be found in clearings and along the edges of virtually all types of forests at all elevations as well as in banana plantations and gardens.

DESCRIPTION	**Adult male**	
	Iris:	brown
	Bill:	decurved; dull black
	Pileum:	dull green
	Loral and ear regions and sides of neck:	bright metallic magenta-purple
	Hind neck to lesser wing coverts:	metallic copper
	Lower back to upper tail coverts:	dull green-bronze, with copper tint
	Underparts:	velvety black, glossed with blue-green and white patches on flanks and base of vent
	Greater wing coverts:	dusky bronze
	Wings:	dusky, with the secondaries faintly glossed with bronze-green
	Under tail coverts:	strongly glossed with green
	Tail:	rounded
	middle pair:	varies from dusky green-bronze to dull black
	remaining pairs:	metallic violet with dark blue-green tips
	Feet:	dusky
	Adult female	Similar to adult male except
	Coloration:	duller, especially black underparts
	Tail:	tipped with pale gray
	Immature male	Similar to the adult female except
	Throat:	deep blue

Female Jamaican Mango
(Anthracothorax mango). *Crystal Spring, Jamaica.*

MEASUREMENTS	*Length:*	5.0 in.
	Wing:	2.75–3.0 in.
	Tail:	1.7 in.
	Bill:	1.1 in.

WEIGHTS	8.5 g
VOICE	A series of staccato "tic-tic-tics."
COURTSHIP	Data not available.
NESTING	The nest, which is made of densely woven silky fibers and cobwebs and adorned with flecks of lichens, holds two white eggs that measure approximately 15.5 mm x 10 mm.

The immature male Jamaican Mango has a deep blue throat that will eventually turn black.

*The Jamaican Mango hummingbirds
found in Crystal Spring feed on red
ginger, hibiscus flowers, and orchids.*

Male Jamaican Mango/Orchid Tree (Bauhinia variegata)

Male Jamaican Mango/Wild Plantain (Heliconia bihai). *Hummingbirds sometimes drink rainwater that has collected in the petals of this flower.*

Male Puerto Rican Emerald
(Chlorostilbon maugaeus). Note:
Back view shows bird feeding from
Parrot's Plantain (Heliconia
psittacorum). *El Yunque, Puerto Rico.*

Puerto Rican Emerald

It is believed by country people in Puerto Rico that the nests of hummingbirds are effective in the treatment of asthma attacks. In some areas the nest is burned and the ashes used to brew a tea then served to the sufferer, in others the nest is simply hung from a string around the neck.

Herbert A. Raffaele
A Guide to the Birds of Puerto Rico and the Virgin Islands
1983

GENUS	*Chlorostilbon*
SPECIES	*Chlorostilbon maugaeus*
ORIGIN OF SCIENTIFIC NAME	*chlorostilbon:* *chloro* (Greek)—green *stilbon* (Greek)—glitter
	maugaeus: Named in honor of M. Mauge.
LOCAL NAMES	Colibrí, Fork-tailed Hummingbird, Zumbador, Zumbadorcito, Zumbadorcito de Puerto Rico, Zunzún
RANGE:	Resident on Puerto Rico.
	Puerto Rico—Adjuntas, Mayagüez, Lares, Ponce, El Yunque, Utuado, Guánica, Maricao Forest, Carite Forest, Caribbean National Forest, Cayey, El Verde, Toro Negro, Río Mameyes, Manatí, Salinas, Juana Diaz, Yauco, Cabo Rojo, Ciales, Aibonito, Hacienda Catalina
HABITAT	As this species prefers the shade, it is very common in montane forests and coffee plantations. It can also be found in open country as well as coastal mangroves.

DESCRIPTION **Adult male**

Iris:	dark brown
Bill:	straight; upper portion is dull black and lower portion is pinkish with a black tip
Upperparts:	dark metallic bronze-green
Chest:	deeper green than the underparts
Underparts:	metallic gold-green
Wings:	dusky, faintly glossed with violet
Tail:	deeply forked; glossy blue-black
Feet:	dusky

Adult female

Iris:	similar to male
Bill:	straight; dull black
Loral and eye regions:	dusky
Upperparts:	metallic green-bronze
Underparts:	pale gray
Sides and flanks:	metallic green
Wings:	dusky, faintly glossed with violet
Tail:	can be forked, emarginate, or slightly double-rounded
middle pair:	metallic green with blue-black tips
second pair:	bronze-green with black tips

Female Puerto Rican Emerald
(Chlorostilbon maugaeus). *Carite Forest, Puerto Rico.*

third pair:	similar, but with more black and a gray spot on the inner web
fourth pair:	half bronze-green at the base with broad blue-black stripe; large spot of pale gray at the tip
outermost pair:	similar, but with an even larger gray spot at the tip
Feet:	dusky

Immature male	Similar to adult male except
Lower bill:	more dusky
Underparts:	darker and duller green

MEASUREMENTS   *Total length:*   3.5 in.

Male		**Female**	
Wing:	1.9 in.	*Wing:*	1.8 in.
Tail:	1.4 in.	*Tail:*	1.1 in.
Bill:	0.5 in.	*Bill:*	0.5–0.6 in.

WEIGHTS   **Male**   3.0–3.4 g   **Female**   2.9–3.6 g

VOICE   The call consists of several "tics" uttered at various speeds. The bird also utters a fast trill that is followed by a shrill hum.

COURTSHIP   Data not available.

NESTING   Although most females nest from February to May, some will breed anytime throughout the year. Molting of adults begins in May and June and continues to August.

The nest, a compact structure in the form of a small cup, is composed of dried plant fibers, such as the scales of the tree fern, lined with wild cotton and other soft materials, and dotted with lichens. It is generally built in either low- or medium-sized plants and trees.

The clutch consists of two white eggs, approximately 13 mm × 8 mm in length.

Young male Puerto Rican Emerald in adult plumage.

Male Puerto Rican Emerald takes to the air.

Male Puerto Rican Emerald in torpor.

The hummingbird holds a special place in the folklore of the country people of the Caribbean. In the Dominican Republic, for example, it is believed that an earache can be healed by inserting a small amount of the hummer's nest into the ear. It is also sometimes used to stop the flow of blood (no doubt because its basic component is a cobweb).

Puerto Ricans treat asthma with a tea made from the remains of burned nests, although those afflicted also claim they find relief by wearing the tiny nest as a necklace.

Magical powers are also attributed to the tiny bird. In Jamaica, sorcerers known as obeahs *make charms out of the bodies of hummingbirds and use them to protect banana and yam patches from thieves. And, like Mexicans, some Cubans believe that the most effective love potion is one made from hummers that have been dried and ground up.*

This Puerto Rican Emerald mother built her nest in full view of hikers and tourists who traveled on the path below it.

The nest of the Puerto Rican Emerald is believed by some country people to have medicinal powers.

Male Purple-throated Carib
(Eulampis jugularis). *Lamentin,*
Martinique. Note: *Back view shows*
bird feeding from Bananier
d'Ornament (Musa ornata). *Notice*
also the silhouette of a female Purple-
throated Carib flying by.

108

Purple-throated Carib

The male looks splendid as he sits on a bare twig, basking in the rays of the hot sun, by some steaming forest pathway, his tail widely spread and the sun flashing from his crimson-purple throat and breast and from his golden-green wings and curious steely-blue upper and under tail-coverts, the whole set off by the velvety blackness of the rest of his plumage....

George E. Lodge
"Notes on Some of the West-Indian Humming-birds"
Ibis
1896

Note: This bird was once known as the Garnet-throated Hummingbird, but that name now applies only to *Lamprolaima rhami.*

GENUS	*Eulampis*
SPECIES	*Eulampis jugularis*

ORIGIN OF SCIENTIFIC NAME	*eulampis:*
	    eu (Greek)—beautiful
	    lampis (Greek)—torch, lamp
	    jugularis (Latin)—throat

LOCAL NAMES	Doctor Bird, Ruby-throat In the French West Indies: Colibri, Colibri Falle Rouge, Colibri Gorge Rouge, Colibri Madère, Doctor Carcoo, Fou-Fou Madère, Frou-Frou, Gros Colibri, Madère, Oiseau-Mouche, Oiseau-Mouche à Gorge Rouge
RANGE	Resident on Lesser Antilles, including St. Eustatius, Saba, St. Kitts, Nevis, Antigua, Montserrat, Guadeloupe, Dominica, Martinique, St. Lucia, and St. Vincent. Casual on Barbuda, Desirade, Îles des Saintes, and Bequia. Has been sighted on Barbados and Grenada. Antigua—Body Ponds Montserrat—Wilk's Ghaut, Jubilee Heights, Chance's Summit Guadeloupe—Riflet Dominica—Freshwater Lake, Morne Trois Pitons, Morne Plaisance Martinique—Chemin Bouliqui, Morne Rouge, Colson, La Medaille, Verrier, Lamentin, St. Joseph, Ste. Marie, Gros Morne, side of Mt. Pelée and Le Pitons, Fort-de-France, Forêt des Trois-Ilets, Route de Moutte, Crève Coeur, the summit of Gitons du Carbet. Extremely rare at sea level. St. Lucia—Edmund Forest Reserve, Mt. Gimie, Quilesse, Piton Flore, Forestière St. Vincent—Soufrière, Richmond Valley, Cumberland Valley, Will-Be-Free Grenada—Corinth Estate, St. David's Parish Barbados—Dukes, St. Thomas Parish

Female Purple-throated Carib
(Eulampis jugularis). *The sexes are alike except that the bill of the female is decurved and longer than that of the male. Lamentin, Martinique.*

Immature Purple-throated Carib

HABITAT	Most abundant in undisturbed lowland and mountainous forests at high elevations, but can also be found in gardens at lower elevations.
DESCRIPTION	Sexes alike except bill of the female is decurved and longer than that of the male.

Adult

Iris:	dark brown
Bill:	that of the female is decurved and longer than that of the male; black
Chin, throat, malar region, and chest:	metallic red-purple
Upperparts:	velvety black
Upper tail coverts:	metallic blue-green
Underparts:	velvety black
Wings (above):	bright metallic green
primaries:	more blue-green, with two outermost appearing duller or nearly black
Wing coverts and secondaries:	more gold-green than the wings
Tail:	emarginate; black, glossed with metallic blue-green
Under tail coverts:	bright metallic blue-green
Feet:	dusky

Immature	Similar to adult except
Bill:	shorter than the adult
Throat:	orange or dark red, speckled with orange
Upperparts:	glossed with blue-green or (in younger individuals), mixed with brown

MEASUREMENTS	**Male**		**Female**	
Total length:	4.4–4.6 in.	*Total length:*	4.5 in.
Wing:	2.9 in.	*Wing:*	2.7 in.
Tail:	1.7 in.	*Tail:*	1.5 in.
Bill:	0.8 in.	*Bill:*	1.0 in.

WEIGHTS	**Adult male**	8.7–11.85 g	**Adult female**	7.3–9.9 g
	Juvenile male	8.5–11.25 g	**Juvenile female**	6.45–9.15 g

VOICE	This bird makes a series of high-pitched whistles.
COURTSHIP	*Note:* At a certain point in the courtship behavior of these birds, the male lowers its guard and allows the female to enter and feed from its territory. Thus, it is interesting to note that the females of this species have been found to "prostitute" themselves for food; that is, they may allow males to mate with them in order to be allowed to feed from rich and once-forbidden areas.

Courtship, which takes up to five minutes, begins when a male chases away a female who has wandered into his territory. There may be five or more of these chases, which continue past the boundary line of the male's territory and end with the female immediately turning right around and heading back into his domain. After a while, the male will allow her to feed temporarily from "his" flowers before chasing her away. Finally, he will permit her to stay.

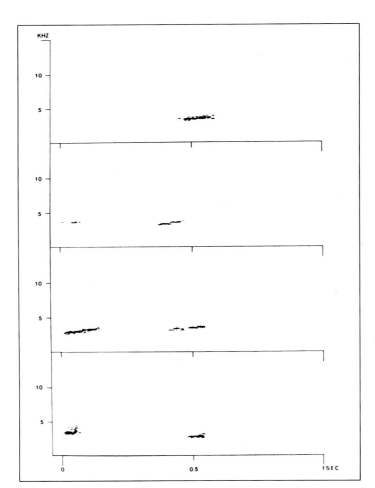

Sound spectrograms of song of male Purple-throated Carib

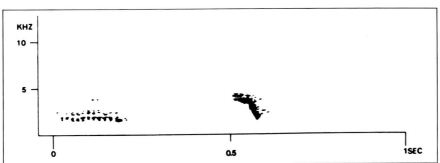

Sound spectrogram of vocalizations of female Purple-throated Carib

Stage 1. Then, about 5 feet from the female, the male, uttering harsh notes, will begin to move to and fro in an "arc-display," holding his wings (or, sometimes, only one wing) away from his body at an angle between 25 and 45 degrees. The pair may then begin to fly from perch to perch in characteristic "jump-flights" accompanied by rustling sounds produced by their wings. The female, who has become bolder by now, may chase the male from any and all of his perches until both ultimately share the same one.

Stage 2. At this point, either the male or the female, bill raised to show off its iridescent throat, will begin to hover about 6 inches away from the other, which sits quietly perched. The sitting bird may swing its head from side to side as it watches the movements of the aggressor and, if it is a male, repeat its earlier horizontal movements or fly around and finally perch on the left and/or right side of the female before trying to mate with her.

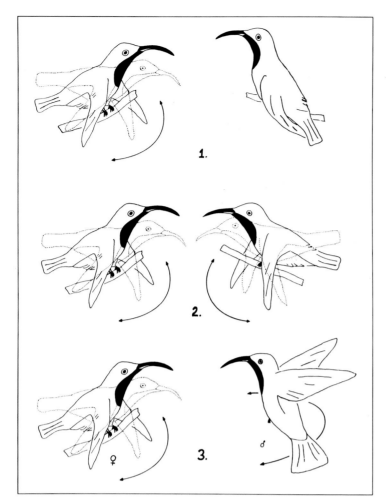

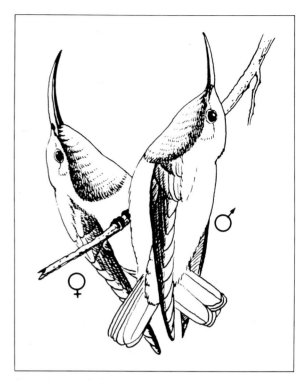

Stage 4—copulation

*Courtship display of the Purple-
throated Carib, Stages 1 to 3*

Stage 3. Sometimes, they may instead fly together slowly, face to face, in an 8-inch circle before attempting to mate.

Stage 4. Mating takes place when the male mounts the female's back or, more commonly, presses his cloaca to hers from the front while both assume a lowered perched position.

After mating, the female may preen slightly on her perch before exiting the area. But she may instead decide to refresh herself by taking a few sips from the flowers the male had once so generously shared with her. Since his ardor has cooled, however, she'll find herself quickly chased out of his territory.

NESTING   This bird, which can breed year-round, generally nests from January to July.

The female will situate her compact nest from 10 to 60 feet from the ground in trees like that of the breadfruit or mango, and build it from thin strips of bark adorned with moss and lichens. Soft plant material, like that of fern leaflets, is used for lining the inside.

The female will sit on her eggs, which measure approximately 15 mm × 11 mm to 16 mm × 10 mm, about 6 minutes at a time for about 63 percent of her day.

A Purple-throated Carib sits on her nest.

The nest of this Purple-throated Carib was built on the side of this branch. Notice the strands of black animal hair lining the top.

Male Purple-throated Carib/Torch Ginger (Etlingera elatior)

Female Purple-throated Carib/
Lobster-claws (Heliconia caribaea)

Male Rufous-breasted Hermit (Glaucis hirsuta). Concord Falls, Grenada.

Rufous-breasted Hermit

The Hairy Hermit is a large, striking brown hummingbird with a very long, deeply curved bill . . . It usually flies with great rapidity but sometimes flits rather slowly through the undergrowth of the forest, appearing very like a diminutive woodcock.

James Bond
Birds of the West Indies
1936

Note: Also called the Hairy Hermit. Very little information of any kind exists for the species on Grenada. Therefore, information on courtship and nesting is taken from studies of the bird in Trinidad and is believed to be similar for both.

GENUS	*Glaucis*
SPECIES	*Glaucis hirsuta*
ORIGIN OF SCIENTIFIC NAME	*glaucis* (Latin)—gray *hirsuta* (Latin)—hairy
LOCAL NAMES	Brown Breast, Brown Doctor Bird, Brown Hummingbird, Colibri Balisier, Doctor Bird
RANGE	Resident on Grenada, Trinidad, and Tobago, as well as the area encompassing central Panama, Colombia, Venezuela, the Guianas, eastern Peru, northern Bolivia, and central Brazil. Grenada—Grand Étang, Concord Falls, Annandale Falls, Halifax Harbor (west coast), Mt. Granby, Morne Delice
HABITAT	Along streambanks in shady mountain forests (at elevations exceeding 1,400 feet), forest edges, and cultivated clearings such as cocoa fields, banana plantations, and nutmeg groves.

DESCRIPTION	**Adult male**	
	Iris:	dark brown
	Bill:	strongly decurved; upper portion is dusky and lower portion is pinkish with dusky tip; streaks of yellow appear on the upper portion of some males
	Pileum:	dull bronze-green
	Chin:	dull white
	Upperparts:	metallic bronze-green
	Abdomen:	pale gray-cinnamon
	Underparts:	dark brown
	Wings:	dusky, faintly glossed with violet
	Upper tail coverts:	broadly tipped with gray
	Tail:	rounded
	middle pair:	metallic bronze-green with narrow white tips
	remaining pairs:	chestnut, with broad black bands and narrow white tips
	Under tail coverts:	pale cinnamon
	Feet:	yellow

Female Rufous-breasted Hermit
(Glaucis hirsuta). *Concord Falls,
Grenada.* Note: *Back view shows bird
feeding from Wild Plantain*
(Heliconia bihai).

Both males and females of this species repeatedly wobble their tails up and down as they perch.

Adult female	Similar to adult male except
Eye region:	prominent white stripe
Underparts:	cinnamon
Tail:	white tips are lighter and broader
Young	Similar to adults except
Pileum:	dusky
Back and rump:	narrowly tipped with gray-buff
Tail:	black bands are broader and tips are narrower

MEASUREMENTS *Length:*

Male	5.1 in.
Female	4.8 in.
Wing:	2.25–2.75 in.
Tail:	1.6 in.
Bill:	1.4 in.

WEIGHTS
Male   7.3 g   **Female**   6.7 g

VOICE   The bird's call, made while it is either perched or in flight, is a single-note "sweep." This is sometimes repeated at length with one- to two-second pauses in between. At times there is a "sweep" followed by several "swee-swees."

COURTSHIP   While sitting on a twig, the male will vibrate and turn his half-opened tail while fluttering his wings and displaying the white feathers of his thighs. The female, who is also perched, may barely flap her wings in response. After a vocal duet with the female, the male will then fly slowly about 4 feet backward and forward in front of her while keeping his head and tail elevated, his feet lowered, and again showing the white feathers of the thigh.

Another duet, followed by a chase, takes place just before

eggs are laid and may also take place prior to mating.

A male can "false mate" by copulating with an object, such as a leaf, instead of a female.

NESTING This bird, which can nest during eight out of the twelve months of the year, often breeds during the first three months of the rainy season and apparently times its nesting period with the blooming season of its favorite blossoms.

Its nest, which is very loosely constructed, is attached with spider webs to the underside of leaves such as those of the fern, wild banana, cocoa tree, or small palm that usually hang over streambeds or trails.

It is made up of fine plant fibers and tiny roots, bound around the leaf into the shape of a cup with long streamers of lichen and bark. Nesting materials include husks of grass seed, shredded bamboo peelings, spiderwebs, and dried moss. The bottom of the nest is so thin that the eggs can easily be seen.

Bits of dried leaves and twigs are used to fashion a tail-like projection that serves to balance it.

The nest, with its curved inner edge and unusually deep interior, is so carefully constructed to ensure the safety of the eggs that when turned upside down, the eggs will usually not tumble out. In addition, the cylindrical shape of the eggs makes it difficult for them to easily roll.

They are built from 2 to 30 feet above the ground, but the majority are found at a height of around 8 feet.

A female can breed either every month or every other month and will often use the same nest again and again, repairing and rebuilding it each time. But she may also raise a second or subsequent brood in a completely new nest situated very near to the first one. One record does exist of a female who built three successive nests.

The clutch consists of two white eggs, each measuring about 15.5 mm × 9.5 mm and weighing around 0.6 grams. They are usually laid forty-eight hours apart during the morning hours, and incubation, which lasts from sixteen to eighteen days, begins only after the second egg has been laid. Incubating females leave the nest more than a dozen times in an eight-hour period and will remain away from the nest from one to ten minutes at a time.
Females are not particularly territorial and will build their nests as close as 7 feet from each other. For this reason, it is not surprising to find two females laying their eggs in the same nest and this accounts for the high ratio of nests that contain three eggs. While it is not uncommon to see them visit each other's nests, they probably will utilize the nest of another only when theirs is damaged or if they fail to finish building their own in time.

This species is unique in that the male stays near the nest during incubation and the early stages of nesting. During

The female attaches its distinctive nest to the underside of leaves. We were once lucky enough to see a female take the first step in constructing her nest when she wrapped a long spiderweb around a fern frond.

this period he helps defend against flycatchers and other hermit hummingbirds who may try to pilfer cobwebs and other materials. From time to time he will even inspect it. When the female is away, he will perch 3 feet from the nest and make his characteristic "chee-call," which is also uttered by both sexes whenever they fly toward the nest. Sometimes he will accompany her when she leaves the nest.

A one-egg clutch also occurs, but has been attributed to a winding down of mating activity as the breeding season nears an end.

Nestlings, with their white downy filaments and black skin, are similar in coloration to that of their nest. After eight days, pinfeathers emerge and start to unfurl in about a week. When hatched, their bills are straight and the upper portion is brownish yellow that soon fades to pure yellow. This starts to turn black after about fourteen days and becomes completely black a week later.

The young chicks remain in their nests from twenty-one to twenty-seven days. Because the babies always face the underside of the leaf to which the nest is attached, the female is forced to hover while she feeds them, about thirteen times a day or from one to two times every hour.

As she hovers, she beats her wings faster, an action that rustles the soft downy feathers of her babies. And the sensation of air moving on the feathers (not the hum created by the increased motion of the wings) stimulates them to gape.

Once her babies have matured, she will feed them while perched on the edge of the nest.

On Grenada, Rufous-breasted Hermits can be found in the rain forest at the Grand Étang Reserve. In the distance is Mt. Sinai (2,307 feet).

Female Rufous-breasted Hermit/Wild Plantain (Heliconia bihai)

124

Male Rufous-breasted Hermit/Wild Plantain (Heliconia bihai)

Rufous-breasted Hermits feed from an abundance of blossoms that grow both in the wild and on a banana plantation near Concord Falls, Grenada.

Male Western Streamertail (Trochilus polytmus). *Kingston, Jamaica.*

Western Streamertail

. . . you can watch him . . . shifting only a fraction of an inch at a time as he probes his coral-red black-tipped beak further into the corolla of the flower; his bronzy-green back and jet-black head exciting your admiration, until it is eclipsed by the blazing emerald of his breast as he suddenly faces you at another flower-head, peering into the blossom with sparkling black eyes . . . surrounded by a filmy grey halo of rapidly vibrating wings, while the two long streamers from his blue-black tail float behind him, gracefully waving at every motion of the bird.

Suddenly he is gone—so quickly, indeed, that you hardly know in which direction this little emerald fairy phantom of an atom has sped his hungry way.

George E. Lodge
"Notes on Some of the West-Indian Humming-birds"
Ibis
1896

Note: The basic differences between the black-billed and red-billed varieties of this bird are the colors of their bills, sexual and aggressive behavior, and the song of the males. Although the American Ornithologists' Union classifies them both as *Trochilus polytmus,* we agree with Dr. Karl-L. Schuchmann that they are different species altogether.

GENUS	*Trochilus*
SPECIES	*Trochilus polytmus*
ORIGIN OF SCIENTIFIC NAME	*trochilus* (Greek)—small bird (wren)
	(*Note:* When Linnaeus first classified hummingbirds, he put all of the known varieties into one single genus called *Trochilus.* Today, of the 116 genera of hummers, only the Western and Eastern Streamertails are left in this original genus.)

	polytmus:
	   poly (Latin)—much
	   tmus (probably from the Latin *thymus*)—spirited

LOCAL NAMES	Doctor Bird, Hummingbird, Jamaican Doctor Bird, Long-tail, Long-tailed Doctor Bird, Long-tailed Hummingbird, Red-billed Streamertail Hummingbird, Scissors-Tail, Streamertail
RANGE	Resident in areas of western Jamaica where the Eastern Streamertail is not found.
Note:	There is one area where both species can be found. This is the region that lies between the Blue Mountains and the John Crow Mountains, bordered by Port Antonio in the north and the Morant River in the south.
HABITAT	Abundant in the forests and mountain zone of the Blue Mountains; common in gardens and parks; seasonal and less abundant in low coastal regions.
DESCRIPTION	**Adult male**
Iris:	dark brown
Bill:	faintly decurved; completely red or red tipped with black
Note:	Bill gets redder as the individual gets older

Male Western Streamertail. Note: *Back view shows bird feeding from Pendant Firebirds* (Heliconia rostrata). *Kingston, Jamaica.*

Crown:	dull black
Nape:	one velvety black crest on either side of the back of the head
Malar region, sides of neck, and underparts:	shining yellow-green
Upperparts:	bright metallic green
Wings:	
primaries:	dark brown, glossed with purple-bronze
Note:	Tenth primary is shorter than the ninth
secondaries:	darker and faintly glossed with violet
Tail:	forked; black
three outer pairs:	scalloped on inner edges
second to outermost pair:	extremely elongated
Note:	They cross when the bird is perched
middle pair:	glossed with bronze-green
all other tail feathers:	also glossed, but in varying degrees
Under tail coverts:	blue-black
Feet:	dusky

Adult female

Iris:	similar to male
Bill:	similar to male
Crown:	dusky gray tipped in metallic green or bronze
Loral and ear region:	dusky gray
Malar region and underparts:	white
Sides of throat:	sometimes spotted with metallic bronze-green
Sides, flanks, sides of neck, and chest:	heavily spotted with metallic bronze-green
Upperparts:	bright metallic bronze-green that gets duller toward the crown
Underparts:	white
Wings:	dusky and faintly glossed with bronze-purple
Note:	Tenth primary is shorter than the ninth
Tail:	double rounded, with no long streamers
outermost tail feathers:	broadly tipped with white
middle pair:	bright bronze-green
all other tail feathers:	black with the portion nearest the body glossed with bronze-green
Feet:	dusky

Immature male — Similar to adult male except

Tail:	no long streamers; tipped with bronze-green
Under tail coverts:	strongly glossed with green-bronze

Male nestling — Similar to immature male except

Crown and back of head:	dusky, faintly glossed with bronze-green; no crest
Overall color:	duller
Underparts:	dull metallic bronze-green

MEASUREMENTS

Male		**Female**	
Length (with streamers):	8.5–10 in.	*Length:*	4.0–4.1 in.
Wing:	2.5–3.0 in.	*Wing:*	2.2–2.3 in.
Tail:		*Tail:*	1.5 in.
streamers:	6.0–7.75 in.	*Bill:*	0.6–1.1 in.
middle feathers:	1.0–1.2 in.		
Bill:	0.7–1.1 in.		

Female Western Streamertail
(Trochilus polytmus). *Kingston,
Jamaica.*

Young male birds, like this one, acquire their distinctive long tail feathers upon reaching adulthood.

*Molting males of this species do not
necessarily drop their long tail
feathers at the same time and can
sometimes be observed with one long
and one short streamer.*

WEIGHTS **Male** 5.2–5.5 g **Female** 4.8 g

VOICE The call is a sharp, metallic "ting" or "teet." The song is a sequence of rapid chirps with a downward inflection, and the conflict call is a descending trill or chatter.

When agitated, the male bird makes a loud single-note "zeet" call that is 370 milliseconds long and has a frequency of 3.5–14.0 kHz.

Its song is composed of the following three-part verse:

1. Three 150-millisecond-long notes sung at a frequency of 3–8 kHz

2. 40-millisecond-long notes sung at a frequency of 3–8 kHz. These are repeated up to 12 times.

3. Long last note sung at a frequency of 3.5–4 kHz

One hears an unusual vibrating sound as the bird is flying. Produced only by males with two fully grown, or almost fully grown, streamers, it is created by the "wavelike" (scalloped) structure of the elongated tail feathers.

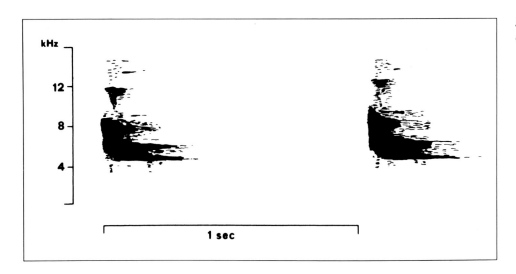

Sound spectrogram of the "zeet" call of the Western Streamertail

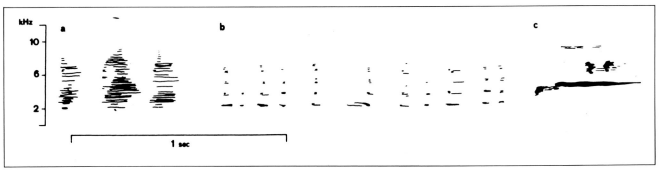

Sound spectrogram of the song of the Western Streamertail

The courtship display of the Western Streamertail, Stages 1 to 3

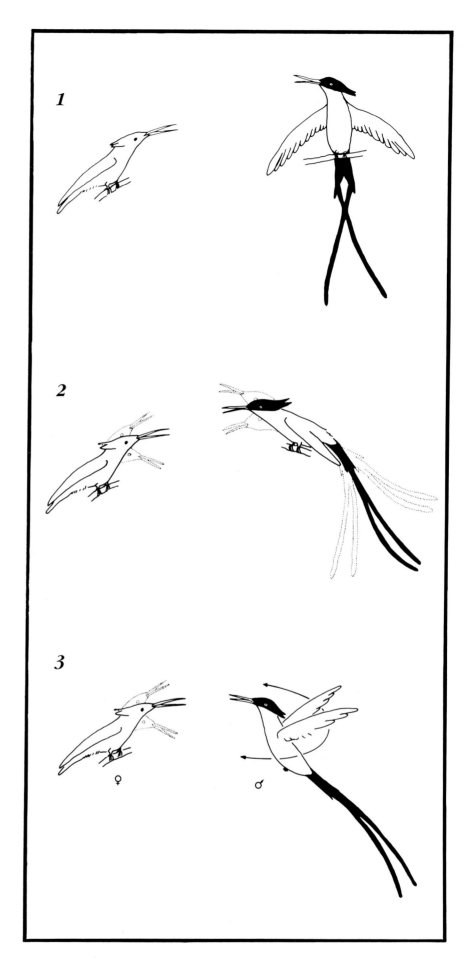

COURTSHIP   *Note:* At the present time, the courtship rituals of approximately two-thirds of the hummingbird family are known. Careful study has revealed that they are made up of

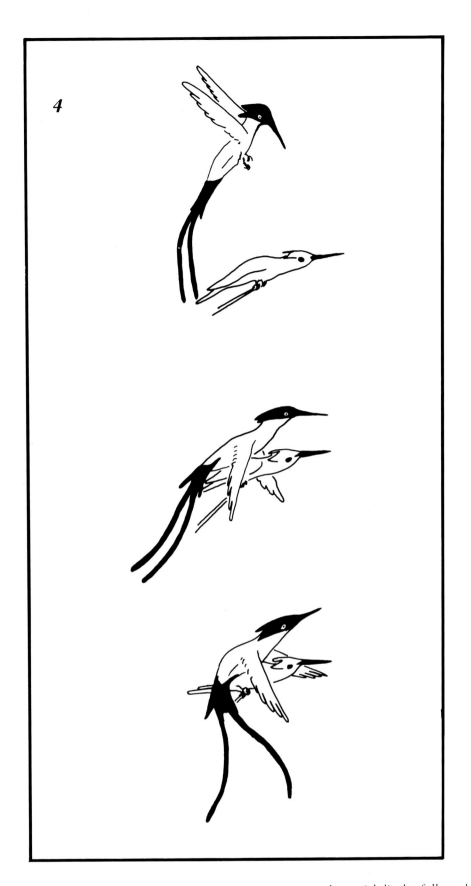

4

two parts—the aerial display followed by copulation. And, although the male generally makes the first move, there are three species that are exceptions to this rule, the Eastern and Western Streamertails and the Long-tailed Hermit, *Phaethornis superciliosus.*

Stage 1. The female flies into the territory of the male, where she will probably be mistaken for an intruder and driven away. When the male finally allows her to perch within his territory, they threaten each other in a very specific manner. From perched positions, the male raises his crest and utters loud "zeet" calls while the female, with beak opened, turns her head and reciprocates with loud "zeets" of her own.

Stage 2. In the next stage, the female allows the male to land on her perch and begins to sharply turn her head from side to side up to an angle of 45 degrees. The male will respond not only by swinging his head but also by turning his tail in both directions. If he does not do this, the female will attack him.

Stage 3. When these swinging movements are synchronized, the male will then fly in front of the female and oscillate his body four to six times in the same direction as her head is turning before approaching her from the side and mounting her. If the synchronized movements of the male and female do not occur, the two birds will revert to their former aggressive behavior.

Stage 4. The birds sing very softly during copulation. And, should the female abandon her perch immediately before mating, the male will proceed to copulate the branch on which she was sitting.

The nest of the Western Streamertail.
Western Foundation of Vertebrate Zoology

NESTING   Females breed from October to March. The female prefers
to nest in low bushes near the forest edge. The compact
nest, which measures about 35 mm in length, is composed
of dry grass, leaves, and other particles of fibrous plants
woven together with cobwebs. The interior measures
approximately 22 mm in depth and about 25 mm in width.
The two eggs are elliptical in shape, and each measures
approximately 14.1 mm × 8.1 mm. The incubation period
ranges from nineteen to twenty-four days. The female has
been known to raise three broods in one breeding season,
often using the same nest.

Breeding in captivity—Cleveland: After one unsuccessful
attempt, a pair of Streamertails finally bred successfully in
captivity at the Cleveland Zoo in 1956.

The female tried out three separate nesting sites before
finally settling upon one that had been fitted with an
artificial nest made of clay and hemp.

She laid two eggs but one was malformed and
subsequently broke while in the nest. The other egg was
broken when the entire nest fell out of the branch.

Less than a month later, she mated with another male and
laid two apparently normal eggs in another nest made by
the keeper. This time, although both eggs hatched, one of
the nestlings died of unknown causes. The other
successfully fledged but was soon attacked by the mother,
at which point they were put into separate enclosures.

Breeding in captivity—Hereford, England: In 1958, an
aviculturist in Hereford, England, noticing that his female
Streamertail was hunting for spiderwebs and other nesting
materials, brought her a male with which to mate.

She laid two eggs in the first nest she had made, but they
broke when the nest fell. She built a second nest directly
on top of the first one, but it was so weakly constructed that
it was necessary to secure it to a plant with a hairnet.

By then the first male had died, so a new one was brought
in, and after copulation the female constructed still a third
nest right on top of the one that still held her two infertile
eggs.

The male, meanwhile, remained on a nearby perch and for
three days aggressively protected her from any birds that
got too close to her or the nest.

Although both eggs hatched successfully, the mother and
one of the nestlings died a few weeks later. The last chick
was hand-fed and thrived until it acquired an eye infection
that greatly weakened it. In any event, it, too, finally died.

Male Western Streamertail/Cardinal's
Guard (Pachystachys spicata)

RED-BREASTED STREAMERTAILS

Thanks to careful observations by members of Jamaica's Gosse Bird Club, interesting peculiarities in the plumage of Streamertails are known.

For example, an adult albinotic, totally white except for its red bill, was spotted in 1972.

And a very rare three-streamered bird was spotted in 1965. This particular bird created such a stir that scientists of the Smithsonian Institution studied it and discovered that it did, indeed, have an additional tail feather. That is, instead of the usual ten feathers, it had eleven, with the extra streamer growing alongside one "normal" one.

Perhaps most interesting of all were the so-called Ruby-throated Streamertails. At the turn of the century, several red-breasted Streamertails were sighted and collected at Up-Park-Camp in the St. Andrews District. These startling birds were again seen at Stony Hill in 1946–47, and in 1973 a pink-breasted female was spotted in the Beverly Hills section of Kingston.

Aberrant individuals of Trochilus polytmus, *these hummingbirds were named* Aithurus taylori, Aithurus *being the former genus of the Streamertail before* Trochilus *was adopted. In the late 1800s several specimens were sent to Lord Rothschild, who officially described it and named it* taylori *in honor of Charles B. Taylor, an early Jamaican naturalist.*

Most of Lord Rothschild's bird collection is now at New York's American Museum of Natural History and there you can see skins of both adults and immature birds. The amount of red on the throats of these different birds ranges from a fairly large round spot to smaller patches of red feathers that emanate from the base of the bill.

These birds were not considered a distinct subspecies of Trochilus polytmus. *Instead, they represented a short-lived "sport," or mutation, of a group of Streamertails found only at Up-Park-Camp and Hope Gardens in the late 1800s and, apparently, later at Stony Hill in the mid-1940s.*

Eastern Streamertail

He drinks in the early morning by sipping the dew, and should we have a shower of rain he extends his wings and flutters them as he sits on a branch of a guava—a favourite tree of his—and sips the rain drops from the leaves.

H. C. Heselton
"Birds of Cuba and Jamaica"
Avicultural Magazine
1903–04

Note: Which came first, the red-billed Streamertail or the black-billed one? Although no one knows for certain, it is believed to have been the latter.

The genus *Trochilus* is thought to be closely related to *Chlorostilbon,* which emerged from the tropical climates of South and Middle America. Only the eastern portion of Jamaica has similar weather, since the rest of the island is subtropical. Therefore, the prevailing theory is that the *black*-billed species was there first.

GENUS	*Trochilus*
SPECIES	*Trochilus scitulus*
ORIGIN OF SCIENTIFIC NAME	*trochilus* (Greek)—small bird (wren)
	(*Note:* When Linnaeus first classified hummingbirds, he put all of the known varieties into one single genus called *Trochilus.* Today, of the 116 genera of hummers, only the Western and Eastern Streamertails are left in this original genus.)
	scitulus (Latin)—beautiful
LOCAL NAMES	Black-billed Streamertail Hummingbird, Doctor Bird, Hummingbird, Jamaican Doctor Bird, Long-tail, Long-tailed Doctor Bird, Long-tailed Hummingbird, Scissors-Tail, Streamertail
RANGE	Resident on eastern Jamaica (the area northeast from the Río Grande River that lies next to the John Crow Mountains and extends southward to the Morant River). Buff Bay, Port Antonio, Cuna Cuna Pass, Bath, Priestman's River, St. Thomas.
	Note: There is one area where both species can be found. This is the region that lies between the Blue Mountains and the John Crow Mountains, bordered by Port Antonio in the north and the Morant River in the south.
	In September of 1988, Hurricane Gilbert destroyed much of the trees and vegetation of eastern Jamaica. Nevertheless, residents of Kingston were surprised to see Eastern Streamertails, blown far from their home, hungrily drinking from feeders alongside their red-billed "cousins"!
HABITAT	Forests, banana plantations, and gardens.
DESCRIPTION	**Adult male**
Iris:	dark brown
Bill:	faintly decurved; black

Male Eastern Streamertail (Trochilus scitulus). *Port Antonio, Jamaica.*

Female Eastern Streamertail (Trochilus scitulus). *Port Antonio, Jamaica.*

Crown:	dull black
Nape:	one velvety black crest on either side of the back of the head

Malar region, sides of neck, and underparts:	shining yellow-green
Upperparts:	bright metallic green
Wings:	dark brown, glossed with purple-bronze
Note:	Tenth primary is shorter than the ninth
inner secondaries:	partly metallic green
Tail:	forked; black
three outer pairs:	scalloped on inner edges
second to outermost pair:	extremely elongated
Note:	They cross when the bird is perched
Under tail coverts:	blue-black
Feet:	dusky

Adult female

Iris:	similar to male
Bill:	similar to male
Crown:	sooty gray tipped with metallic green
Upperparts:	metallic, slightly bronze-green
Sides of neck to flanks:	spotted with metallic green
Underparts:	white
Wings:	dusky, faintly glossed with purple
Tail:	double rounded; no long streamers
two outermost pairs:	broadly tipped with dull white
middle pair:	metallic bronze-green
all other pairs:	blue-black with metallic bronze-green at the base
Feet:	dusky

MEASUREMENTS	**Male**		**Female**	
Length (with streamers):	8.5–9.5 in.		*Length:*	4.0 in.
Wing:	2.5–2.6 in.		*Wing:*	2.1–2.2 in.
Tail:			*Tail:*	1.4–1.5 in.
streamers:	5.75–6.5 in.		*Bill:*	0.8–1.0 in.
middle feathers:	1.1 in.			
Bill:	0.8–0.9 in.			

WEIGHTS	**Male**	6.3 g	**Female**	4.7–4.8 g

VOICE   When excited, this bird makes a loud single-note "zeet" call that is 250 milliseconds long and has a frequency of 3.5–8.0 kHz.

Its song is a verse consisting of stereo notes that range from 150 to 190 milliseconds in length, sung at a frequency of 3–8 kHz. The verse is repeated at will.

One hears an unusual vibrating sound as the bird is flying. Produced only by males with two fully grown, or almost fully grown, streamers, it is created by the "wavelike" (scalloped) structure of the elongated tail feathers.

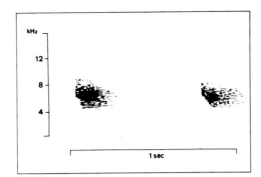

Sound spectrogram of the "zeet" call of the Eastern Streamertail

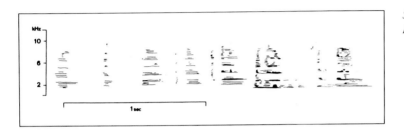

Sound spectrogram of the song of the Eastern Streamertail

COURTSHIP *Note:* At the present time, the courtship rituals of approximately two-thirds of the hummingbird family are known. Careful study has revealed that they are made up of two parts—the aerial display followed by copulation. And, although the male generally makes the first move, there are three species that are exceptions to this rule, the Eastern and Western Streamertails and the Long-tailed Hermit, *Phaethornis superciliosus.*

Stage 1. The female flies into the territory of the male, where she will probably be mistaken for an intruder and driven away. When the male finally allows her to perch within his territory, they threaten each other in a very specific way. From a perched position, the male raises his crest and utters loud "zeet" calls while the female, with beak opened, turns her head and reciprocates with loud "zeets" of her own.

Stage 2. With his bill open and claws extended, the male then flies toward the female, eventually landing on her perch. The female then flies to and fro in front of the male before again sitting on the perch that has been abandoned by the male, who now flies backward. This behavior is repeated four to six times, or until the female demonstrates her readiness to proceed by leaning forward with outspread wings. Should either partner stop the rhythmic flying on and off the perch, the initial aggressive behavior begins again.

Stage 3. The birds sing quietly during copulation. And should the female abandon her perch immediately before mating, the male will copulate the branch.

Stage 2

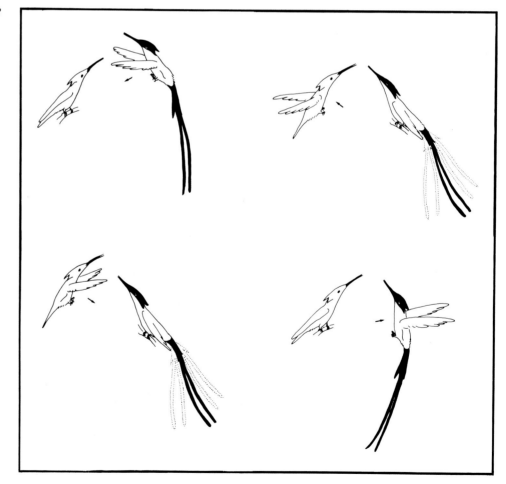

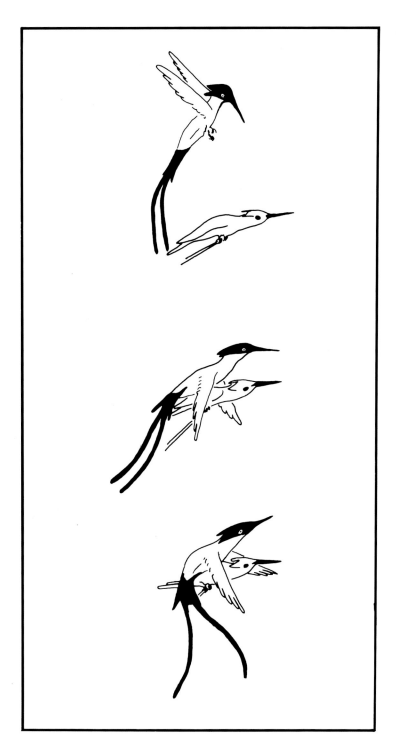

NESTING   Females breed from October to March and favored locations for nest building are at heights of 9 to 13 feet in the secondary growth of the forest. The nest measures about 35 mm × 22 mm × 25 mm and is similar to that of the Western Streamertail. However, instead of delicate fibers, this bird's nests show a preference for coarser components such as tiny twigs, branches, and roots. It is also more loosely constructed, allowing for free drainage of rain through it, an important requirement since this bird resides in the rainiest part of the island. The female lays two elliptically shaped white eggs that are about 13.8 mm × 8.3 mm in size. Eggs are incubated from eighteen to twenty days and multiple broods are possible.

Female Eastern Streamertail/
Asystasia gangetica

*Male Eastern Streamertail/
Pendant Firebirds (Heliconia
rostrata)*

Male Vervain Hummingbird
(Mellisuga minima). Note: *The front
view shows an immature male
Vervain Hummingbird attacking the
perched male. Kingston, Jamaica.*

Vervain Hummingbird

Frequently one . . . will . . . dart . . . upward, looking exactly like a humble-bee. Indeed, the figure of the smaller Hummingbirds on the wing, their rapidity, their arrowy course, and their whole manner of flight, are entirely those of an insect; and one who has watched the flight of a large beetle or bee, will have a very good idea of the form of one of these tropic gems, painted against the sky. . . .

". . . they flocked together . . . "like bees," and the air resounded with their humming, as if in the neighborhood of a hive. . . ."

Philip Henry Gosse
The Birds of Jamaica
1847

GENUS	*Mellisuga*
SPECIES	*Mellisuga minima*
ORIGIN OF SCIENTIFIC NAME	*mellisuga:* 　*melli* (Latin)—honey 　*suga* (Latin)—suck *minima* (Latin)—least (size)
LOCAL NAMES	In Jamaica: Doctor Bird, Little Bee Hummingbird, Little Doctor Bird In the Dominican Republic: Zumbadorcito, Zumbaflor In Haiti: Ouanga Négresse, Sucé-Fleurs
RANGE	Resident on Jamaica and Hispaniola (Dominican Republic and Haiti) and the nearby islands of Gonâve and Tortue, Saona and Catalina islands, and Île-à-Vache; accidental in Puerto Rico. Jamaica—Kingston, Spanish Town, Priestman's River, Port Henderson, Hope Gardens Dominican Republic—Santo Domingo, Bonao, Sánchez, La Vega, Jarabacoa, Puerto Plata, Samaná, Constanza, Honduras, Cana Honda, La Canita, San Francisco Mountains, Río San Juan Haiti—Cavaillon, St. Marc, Pétionville, Gloré, Trou Caïman, Jérémie, Trou-des-Roseaux, Port-au-Prince, Fonds-des-Nègres, La Cahobes, Hinche, Caracol, L'Acul, Fort Liberté
HABITAT	Common in all areas with the exception of dense forests.

DESCRIPTION	**Adult male**	
	Iris:	dark brown
	Bill:	straight; dull black
	Chin and throat:	sometimes flecked with gray or dull bronze
	Upperparts:	dull metallic bronze-green, usually darker or duller on the top of head
	Underparts:	dull white (purer white on chest and abdomen)
	Sides and flanks:	metallic bronze-green
	Wings:	dusky, faintly glossed with violet
	Tail:	emarginate

Female Vervain Hummingbird
(Mellisuga minima). Note: *The front
view shows the bird perched on the
tip of a bract from a maguey plant.
Kingston, Jamaica, and Jarabacoa,
Dominican Republic.*

middle pair:	metallic bronze-green, darker (sometimes blackish) near the tip
remaining pairs:	black, faintly glossed with blue or green
Under tail coverts:	sometimes with a central spot of gray-bronze
Feet:	dusky

Adult female	Similar to male except
Underparts:	plain whitish
Tail:	rounded
two outermost pairs:	broadly tipped with white
third pair:	usually with small white or gray-white tips

Immature male	Similar to adult female except
Chin and throat:	flecked with dusky color
Tail:	
outer tail feathers:	white tips not as sharply defined

MEASUREMENTS	*Length:*	2.5 in.
	Wing:	1.4–1.8 in.
	Tail:	0.75 in.
	Bill:	0.4 in.

WEIGHTS **Male** 2.6–2.7 g **Female** 2.2–3.6 g **Immature male** 2.3 g

VOICE   The song, which has a definite rhythm, consists of a series of high-pitched metallic squeaks and is quite loud considering the diminutive size of bird. The bird sometimes also makes a lengthy, guttural buzzing sound.

Immature male Vervain Hummingbird

Hummingbirds are solitary birds and do not like to share perches. Here, a Vervain Hummingbird aggressively forces another to move down from its original perch.

COURTSHIP *Stage* 1. With widespread tails and while noisily chattering to each other, both male and female quickly rise straight up into the air to a height of more than 60 feet. When they reach the top they close their tails, stop their singing, and hover quietly for a brief moment. Each then slowly glides down in separate flight paths that gradually take them farther and farther apart until they almost reach the ground. They can repeat this display as many as twenty times in a row.

Stage 2. Copulation takes place when the male mounts the female and they fly in a straight line very low to the ground for a distance of about 80 feet.

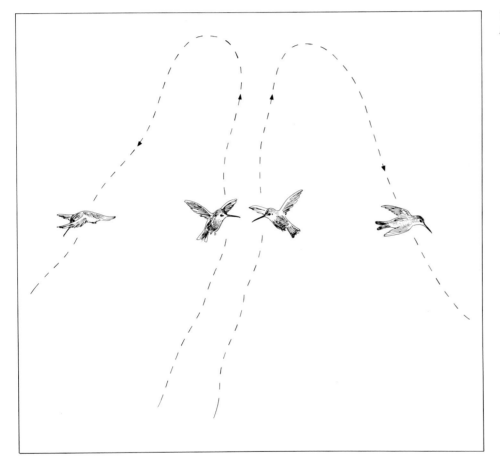

The courtship display of the Vervain Hummingbird, Stage 1

Stage 2—copulation

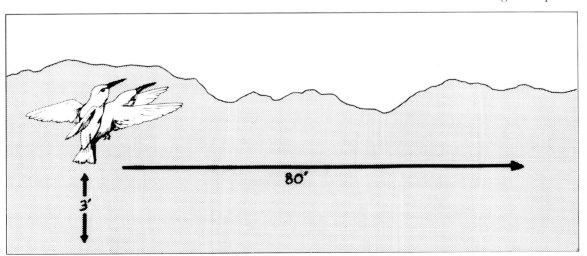

80'

3'

NESTING Two white eggs are laid in minute, tightly woven cups made of cottony fibers that are sometimes flecked with lichens, moss, cobwebs, silk from cocoons, and bark. Proportionately speaking, the eggs, which resemble those of the Antillean Crested Hummingbird, are large (about 11.6 mm × 8.4 mm) and the two can make up an astonishing 34 percent of the mother's total body weight. Nesting sites, which are often low to the ground, include lantana and guava bushes as well as the smooth shoots of the bamboo plant. Incubation lasts about twelve days and, once hatched, the young chicks remain in the nest from nineteen to twenty-two days.

Nests of the Vervain Hummingbird. Clockwise, Jarabacoa, Dominican Republic; Kingston, Jamaica; Tortuga Island, Haiti.

If the mother abandons her nest, or is killed, the unfortunate nestling will perish. Jardin Botánico Nacional Dr. Rafael M. Moscoso, Dominican Republic

This tiny female Vervain Hummingbird perches delicately on the slender tip of a bromeliad. Jardin Botánico Nacional Dr. Rafael M. Moscoso, Dominican Republic

*Male Vervain Hummingbird/Coral
Plant* (Russelia equisetiformis).
Kingston, Jamaica.

Immature male Vervain Hummingbird/Japanese Hat (Holmskioldia sanguinea). *Kingston, Jamaica.*

Male Vervain Hummingbird/Flame of the Woods (Ixora coccinea)

*The hummingbird has the greatest
flight capabilities of any bird. Bee
Hummingbird. Playa Larga, Ciénega
de Zapata, Cuba.*

Anatomy, Food, Feathers, and Flight

4

ANATOMY

Besides their minute size, hummingbirds stand apart from other birds in other anatomical ways. Some of these peculiarities include:

Bills. One of the hummingbird's most notable characteristics is its long, needlelike bill. It can be straight, decurved, or even curved upward. And although more than 80 percent are dusky-black, some are red or even yellow. Usually longer than the head, those of male birds are often shorter than those of the females.

They range in size from 4 inches for the aptly named Sword-billed Hummingbird (whose bill is nearly as long as its body) to the tiny 5/16-inch bill of the Purple-backed Thornbill.

The great diversity in both length and shape is directly related to the bird's feeding habits. Most of the flowers that hummingbirds feed from are long and tubular with ample supplies of nectar situated deep within. Thus, a long, thin bill is necessary to reach the center of these special blossoms. But many flowers have evolved to accommodate the most diverse hummers. For example, those that the Sword-billed Hummingbird feeds from are extremely long while the White-tipped Sicklebill's strongly decurved bill enables it to feed from blossoms that have an equally exaggerated curvature. There's even a Tooth-billed Hummingbird, whose beak, lined with tiny, sharp, toothlike projections, enables it to easily eat the insects that make up the main part of its diet.

Tongue. The hummingbird is capable of harvesting nectar from deep within a long, tubular flower because it has an extra-long tongue.

Like that of the woodpecker, the hummer's translucent tongue is controlled by the hyoid apparatus, a muscle that rests around the back of the bird's skull. Halfway down its length, the tongue divides into two parts, each of which ends in a pointed tip. These tips may have feathery fringes on them that are useful in catching tiny insects that live deep within a flower.

Contrary to popular belief, hummingbirds do not suck in nectar, but collect it instead with a licking motion at a rate of about 13 licks per second.

Hummingbird bills come in a variety of shapes and sizes. (1) Sword-billed Hummingbird, (2) White-tipped Sicklebill, (3) Fiery-tailed Awlbill, (4) Purple-backed Thornbill, (5) Tooth-billed Hummingbird.

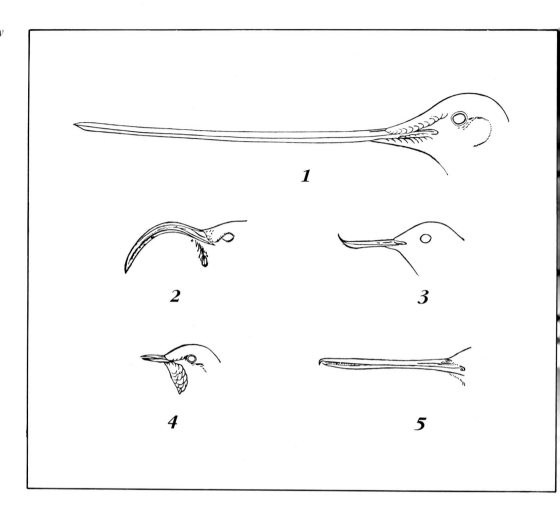

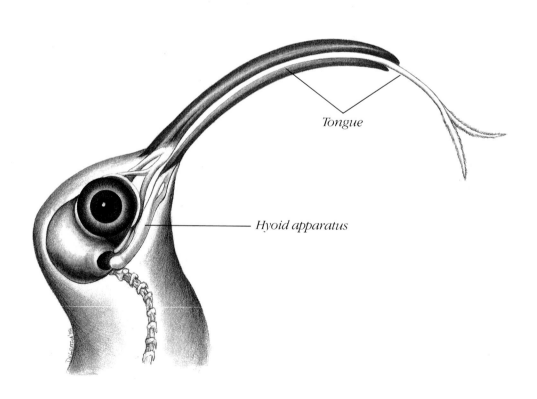

Hummingbirds use their extensile forked tongues to reach nectar reserves deep within flowers.

Digestive System.   The hummingbird consumes the greatest amount of food, relative to its body weight, of any vertebrate. And compared to other birds, it not only has the fastest metabolism, but important differences in its digestive system as well.

For example, it does not have a gizzard, or that part of the stomach that usually holds sand or gravel to grind food. It simply isn't necessary for a bird that feeds solely on nectar and insects. Also, the interior of the stomach itself is soft, not hard like those of other birds.

In addition, the hummingbird does not have either a gallbladder or caeca, finger-like projections located between both intestines that aid digestion.

Circulatory System.   Relatively speaking, the heart of the hummingbird is the largest of all animals and ranges from 1.75 to 2.5 percent of its total body weight. When resting, its heart beats about 500 times per minute and rises to over 1,200 times per minute if the bird becomes excited. Its typical daytime temperature is about 105 degrees F.

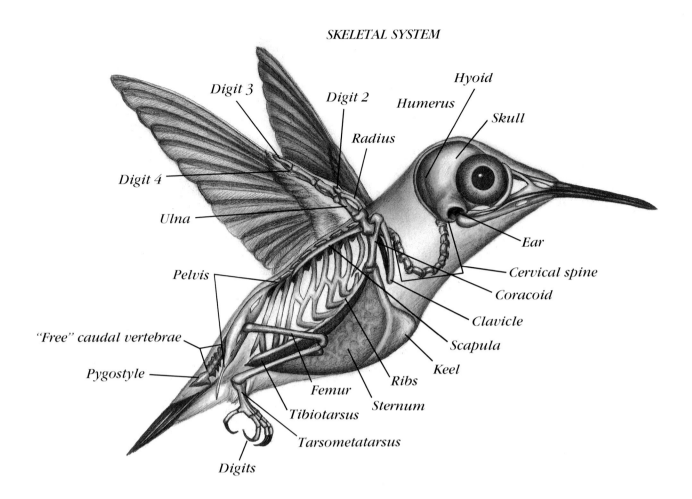

Skeleton. The hummingbird has a total of eight pairs of ribs, two pairs more than most birds. Its sternum, or breastbone, is considerably deep and is also the largest, proportionately, in the entire class of birds, running nearly the entire length of the bird's body. This unusual dimension provides a greater area for the attachment of the bird's powerful flight muscles.

Of particular importance is the structure of the bird's arm, for it differs in size from that of other birds. Most birds have a long upper arm (humerus), a long forearm (radius and ulna), and a short hand. The hummingbird, however, has a short upper arm, short forearm, and a considerably long hand. This anatomical adaptation contributes to the hummingbird's swift wingstroke.

FOOD

Hummingbirds appear to be in constant motion. Their wings seem to be beating a mile a minute as they hover, streak across the sky, or merely dart from one flower to another. Actually they spend a great deal of their time perched quietly, but there is a great deal of activity going on *inside* their bodies, because, like shrews, they have one of the fastest metabolic rates among animals.

In fact, if a man's metabolic rate were as high as that of a hummingbird, he would probably have to consume two times his body weight, or around 155,000 calories, daily in food. That's equal to 285 pounds of hamburger, or 370 pounds of potatoes, or 130 pounds of bread. In addition, his temperature would be 750 degrees F.! What kind of food must a hummingbird consume in order to keep its extraordinary internal

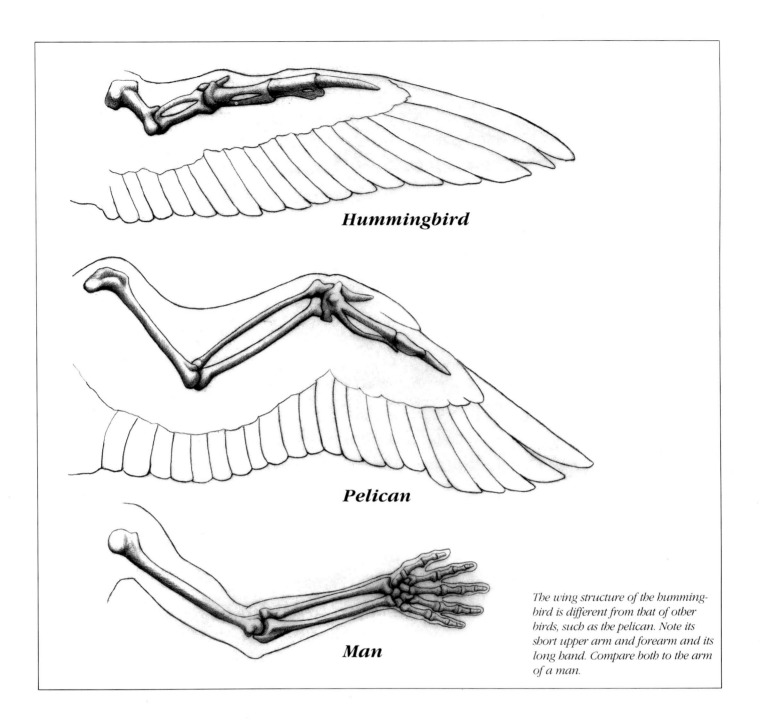

Hummingbird

Pelican

Man

The wing structure of the hummingbird is different from that of other birds, such as the pelican. Note its short upper arm and forearm and its long hand. Compare both to the arm of a man.

furnace stoked? Well, although there is an isolated report of a Jamaican Mango feeding from a plastic cup filled with sugar *granules,* the hummer relies on nectar, an excellent source of quick energy that is easily digested.

So necessary is this sugary liquid, in fact, that the bird may consume up to 50 percent of its weight in nectar every day.

For many years, naturalists and aviculturists unwittingly killed hummingbirds while attempting to keep them in captivity on a diet composed solely of honey. Indeed, there are countless sad accounts of these delicate birds dying aboard ship en route to Europe and America because information concerning their diets was not known.

It wasn't until the early nineteenth century that it was learned that invertebrates such as insects and tiny spiders were an essential part of the bird's diet as well.

Some hummers, like the Western Streamertail, are sometimes seen poking their

The metabolic rate of the hummingbird, one of the fastest of all animals, is fueled by flower nectar. Male Antillean Crested Hummingbird/Red Ginger (Alpinia purpurata). *Grand Étang, Grenada.*

bills into fruits as well as into holes made by the Yellow-bellied Sapsucker in eucalyptus trees. Others fly directly into the midst of insect swarms or pick minute creatures from within the corollas of flowers and along tree trunks. They have also been observed hovering near the webs of spiders, rarely tearing the fragile silk or becoming entangled. They thus are able to dine not only on the unfortunate victims trapped in the cobweb, but often on the spider itself.

This Bee Hummingbird slowly goes into torpor. Playa Larga, Ciénega de Zapata, Cuba.

Early observers were curious enough about the bird's eating habits to perform rudimentary investigations. One such individual, George Lodge, noted in 1896: "One of these birds had a mass of minute black insects in its crop. I put this mass into water, and on examination through a strong magnifying-glass it appeared to be composed entirely of very small black ants, each having two pairs of longish wings. There were several dozens of them. That the birds do suck nectar out of flowers is true enough, but they find their staff of life in insects."

An exact scientific evaluation of the hummingbird's digestive system provides a better look into just what these birds do eat.

The stomach contents of several Puerto Rican hummingbirds have been carefully studied and reveal the importance of animal protein. Nectar measurements are not included in the analyses, but, as mentioned before, nectar is a vital part of their diet.

The stomachs of several Antillean Crested Hummingbirds were composed of 100 percent animal matter, such as spiders, flies, ants, and parasites. Puerto Rican Emeralds had substantial amounts of sand and dirt, a large number of spiders, and a small amount of lantern flies and mosquitos. Those of the Green-throated Carib were interesting because in addition to lantern flies, leaf hoppers, beetles, weevils, other tiny insects, and spiders there were also tiny bits of vegetable matter.

And 98 percent of the stomach contents of the Green Mango was found to contain spiders, engraver beetles, leaf beetles, weevils, ants, flies, and other insects. The remainder was made up of seeds and vegetable scraps. One particularly curious aspect of the digestive habits of this bird has to do with its method of expelling waste material in the form of pellets approximately 2 millimeters in length by 1 millimeter in width. Careful examination of these pellets showed they were made up of chitinous bits of spiders and insects.

Like the Green Mango, the Puerto Rican Mango's solid food consists of about two percent plant material and 98 percent animal protein. The latter takes the form of lantern flies, leaf hoppers, snout, deathwatch, and leaf beetles, earwigs, ants, and spiders.

When a hummingbird has not fed adequately throughout the day, it may enter a comalike state called torpor during which its heart and breathing rates slow down.

In the late 1800s, fashionable ladies were fond of feather fans decorated with tiny hummingbirds. The Fine Arts Museum of San Francisco.

FEATHERS

If a hummingbird can be called beautiful, it's because of its iridescent plumage. Lustrous and shining, it reflects light as does the most expensive sparkling jewel. In fact, throughout history the hummingbird has earned the name "feathered jewel." Unfortunately, the glittering quality of its plumage made the tiny bird the perfect ornament to adorn bonnets, feathered fans, and even satin evening shoes in the late 1800s.

Hummingbirds so captured the fancy of both European and American women that fashion designers and milliners, hard pressed to churn out enough accessories to satisfy the demands of their well-heeled clients, turned to professional dealers to provide them with the necessary skins.

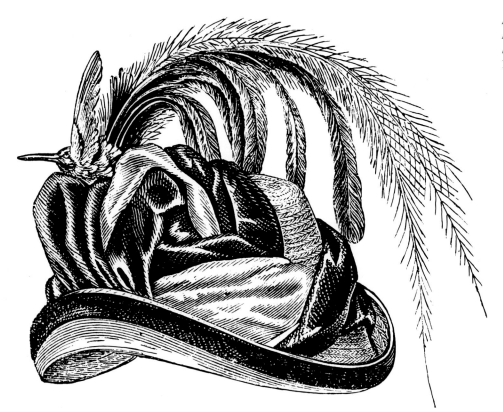

Santa Fé de Bogotá and other South American cities like Rio de Janeiro were the major export centers where consignments as large as 12,000 skins were not unusual. European capitals such as London were the sites of the subsequent sales, like the one in 1888 in which an astonishing 400,000 hummingbirds and other North and South American birds exchanged hands.

Structure. What makes the hummingbird feather shine so brightly? Well, early naturalists believed that the fiery glow was caused by mysterious substances carried in the bird's bloodstream. Today we know that the iridescence is created by interference, a process that produces colors in thin films like soap bubbles and oil slicks.

Feathers have tiny extensions called barbules that give them their weblike quality. Barbicels are the even tinier projections that extend from the barbules.

The top third of an iridescent feather of a hummingbird has no barbicels. Instead, its barbules contain platelets, tiny elliptical structures, that vary in size and contain air bubbles. It is the combination of the thickness of the platelet and the amount of air inside that determines the color.

What strikes people who see our pictures of hummingbirds for the first time are the sparkling ruby, sapphire, or emerald throats and crowns. And time and again we hear them sadly say, "All of the hummingbirds in my backyard are green or gray."

We try to explain that the hummingbirds in their yards may very well be in full, dazzling plumage. The problem is that iridescent feathers are harder to see.

These feathers have barbules that are even more specialized. They are flat and mirrorlike, and allow light hitting them to be reflected in only one direction. To see the brilliant hues you must have the bird directly in front of you and the sun directly behind you. If you, the bird, or the sun are not in exact alignment, the hummingbird will appear dusky green, violet, or even red. When no light shines on it, it looks black.

The iridescent feathers of the hummingbird must be viewed from an exact angle in order to see them sparkle. Otherwise some of the feathers will appear dark. Antillean Crested Hummingbird, Concord Falls, Grenada.

But the barbules on the feathers of the bird's back are concave and allow light hitting them to be reflected in all directions. This explains why the bird's back always glows, but much less brilliantly. And since the backs of most North American hummingbirds are green, it also explains why this is the only color most people see.

The iridescent feathers are an important example of adaptive coloration and do two things—conceal and attract. By being difficult to see unless from a very specific angle, the feathers protect it from sharp-eyed enemies because, from the back, perched hummingbirds look just like leaves on a tree. At the same time, the conspicuous glitter of the male's feathers attracts the attention of a female during a nuptial dive.

FLIGHT

The hummingbird has the most superior flight capabilities of any bird. It can fly forward, backward, to the right and to the left, hover, rise straight up into the air, and even fly upside down. It relies on its powers of flight to such an extent that its tiny feet are virtually useless for anything except perching. Even if it must move a distance of an inch or two, it will probably fly.

Its powerful flight muscles are so important that they make up an incredible 25 to 30 percent of the bird's total weight. But there's another secret to their aerial acrobatics—they utilize a different kind of flying technique.

For example, the upstroke in other birds is relatively unimportant since they rely so strongly on the downstroke to propel them. But to the hummingbird both upstroke and downstroke are equally important, as proven by the fact that the muscles

The wings of the hummingbird trace specific patterns as the bird makes different flight maneuvers. From top to bottom, forward flight, backward flight, and hovering.

controlling these movements are nearly identical in size. This is highly unusual since the upstroke muscles of other birds weigh only 5 to 10 percent of the downstroke muscles.

The hummingbird's method of flying is also different in that, unlike other birds, it cannot flex its wing at all at the elbow or wrist joint. Instead, the wing moves only at the shoulder where it rotates almost 180 degrees. When flying forward, the wings trace a vertical oval in the air; when flying backward, they trace a horizontal circle above its body; and when hovering, they form a figure eight.

The bird is famous for its whirring wings that beat faster than the eye can see, and special cinematic techniques developed to make it possible to actually count these wingbeats proved one thing—the smaller the wing, the faster the wingbeat. For example, birds with wings measuring 1.3 to 2.1 inches had wingbeats of 38 to 78 times per second and those whose wings measured 2.5 to 3.4 inches had wingbeats of 18 to 28 times per second.

How fast do they fly? Well, small ones like the Ruby-throated Hummingbird fly approximately 45 to 55 mph, while the larger Blue-throated or Long-tailed Sylph fly at speeds of 30 to 47 mph.

Hummingbirds can fly straight up into the air like helicopters. Immature male Purple-throated Carib. Lamentin, Martinique.

Hummingbirds can stop suddenly and land lightly because of the small amount of momentum they create. Female Bahama Woodstar, Nassau, Bahamas.

Nature's Helicopter.   Because of its remarkable aerial capabilities, the hummingbird is sometimes called "Nature's helicopter."

The aviation community is well aware of the hummingbird's flight wizardry. The logo of the American Helicopter Society, for example, is a hummingbird. And in 1940, the German Navy utilized the Flettner F1 282 Kolibi (Humming Bird), a helicopter considered to be the most maneuverable of any built during World War II. Used for antisubmarine warfare, it caught the attention of the Luftwaffe, which, together with the Navy, orderd an amazing 1,000 helicopters into production. The Allies, however, bombed the Munich factory in which they were being manufactured and they were never completed.

Until recently, no aircraft was capable of matching the flight ability of the hummer. Helicopters could match all of its maneuvers except that of flying upside down. Today, the bird has finally met its match. There are now two different helicopters that can claim the distinction of flying upside down. They are the Messerschmidt BO-105, a light model manufactured by Messerschmidt Boelkow Blohm, and the medium-weight McDonnell/Douglas U.S. Army AH-64A Apache attack helicopter. Both are capable of doing loops and rolls.

*When startled, this female Western
Streamertail suddenly backed away.
Kingston, Jamaica.*

You can attract hummingbirds to your home by hanging a colorful feeder filled with a simple sugar solution. Feeders courtesy of Perky-Pet Products, Inc., Denver, Colorado

You can attract hummingbirds to your home by using an inexpensive feeder that can be easily found in drugstores, supermarkets, nurseries, and pet stores.

Fill it with a solution of four parts water to one part sugar, a proportion that is equal to the sugar concentration of the hummingbird's favorite blossoms. Don't use honey because it ferments and causes a fungus on the bird's tongue from which it may not recover.

Boil the water first, since this helps the sugar dissolve more easily and discourages the growth of bacteria. By the way, we've learned that there are well-meaning individuals who believe that sugar is bad for humans and, therefore, bad for hummingbirds, too. They fill their feeders with Nutrasweet and Saccharin, not realizing that these substances are non-nutritive and, therefore, capable of quite literally "starving" a hummer to death.

Manufacturers of feeders know that the hummer's favorite color is red and that's why the containers are usually painted red or have red accents. For this reason, it really isn't necessary to add red food coloring to your sugar solution.

Be sure to clean the feeder once a week by soaking it in a bucket of soapy water to which a tablespoon of bleach has been added. Scrub well, perhaps using a bottle brush, and be sure to rinse thoroughly.

Since bees, wasps, and other flying insects also love to drink nectar and can therefore be a problem, try one of the "drip free" feeders to discourage them. And to keep ants from invading feeder holes, coat the wire from which the feeder is suspended.

*Male Purple-throated Carib/Bananier
d'Ornement* (Musa ornata).
Martinique.

Wildflower Pollination 5

Created to live in a perfumed atmosphere of . . . blossoms, they are found continually buzzing around their petals, stopping suspended as if enchanted, in front of each one, like the twilight butterflies. . .

J. Lambeye
Aves de la isla de Cuba
1850

The hummingbird's role in nature is to cross-pollinate flowers with pollen that it carries on its crown, throat, and bill. It comes into contact with the powdery substance while hovering in front of a blossom as it feeds. However, some hummers will rest whenever possible while feeding by perching on the petals. The Bee Hummingbird has even been observed holding on to the stamens of the hibiscus while drinking nectar before moving on to the next flower.

In order to lure hummingbirds to them, these flowers produce nectar, which is generally located deep within the blossom. The bird harvests it by inserting its long bill and extending its tongue to reach it.

Unlike some insects, the hummingbird is not attracted to flowers by scent. Instead, it selects blossoms on the basis of color, preferring those in the warmer shades of the spectrum.

Red flowers with tubular corollas generally produce a greater quantity of nectar than other flowers, an aspect that is important to a bird that burns a lot of energy. In addition, competition for nectar from these blooms is reduced significantly since not only are they odorless (and, therefore, not conspicuous to insects), but insects, with the exception of butterflies, do not readily see the color red.

This explains why hummers seek out objects that are red—not only flowers but also crimson hats, clothes, and even polished fingernails!

Hummingbirds forage, or search for food, in several ways. For example, those that are *territorial* migrate to specific locations abundant in flowers that produce copious quantities of nectar.

Others, known as *trapliners,* do not establish territories, choosing instead to feed from flowers found in the extensive areas over which they roam. Still others are known as *residents.* They remain in an area year-round and vigorously defend their territories from any invaders.

NECTAR ROBBERS

Some species of Caribbean hummingbirds tap nectar in a different way. In addition to certain bees, birds like the bananaquit are known as "nectar robbers." They feed on nectar without pollinating the plant and compensate for their inability to reach deep into the flower by actually drilling holes close to the base, gaining access to the sugary liquid in that way.

Hummingbirds cross-fertilize flowers with pollen carried on their crowns, bills, and throats. Female Vervain Hummingbird/Coral Plant (Russelia equisetiformis). *Santo Domingo, Dominican Republic.*

These drawings of hummingbird heads and flowers show how flowers have adapted both in length and shape to the bills of the birds that feed from them.

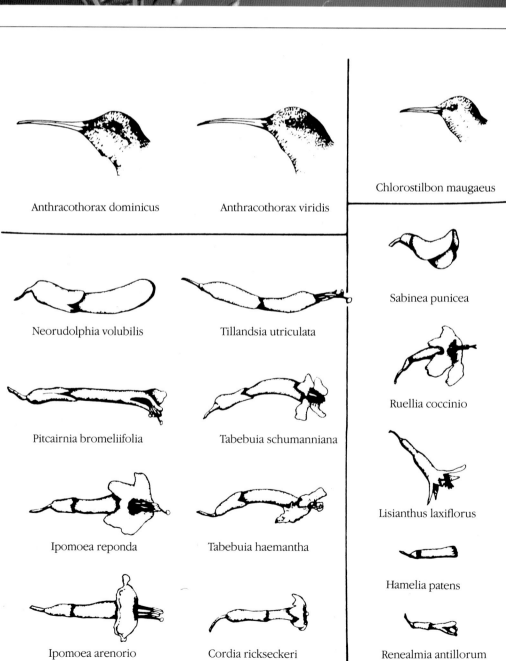

Anthracothorax dominicus

Anthracothorax viridis

Chlorostilbon maugaeus

Neorudolphia volubilis

Tillandsia utriculata

Sabinea punicea

Pitcairnia bromeliifolia

Tabebuia schumanniana

Ruellia coccinio

Ipomoea reponda

Tabebuia haemantha

Lisianthus laxiflorus

Hamelia patens

Ipomoea arenorio

Cordia rickseckeri

Renealmia antillorum

Not all hummers hover while feeding. Some prefer to cling to petals to conserve energy. Male Puerto Rican Emerald/Parrot's Plantain (Heliconia psittacorum) *and male Purple-throated Carib/Pendant Firebirds* (Heliconia rostrata)

*Some hummingbirds tap nectar from the base of the flower. Because they do not aid in the blossom's fertilization, they are known as "nectar robbers." Male Cuban Emerald/*Barleria cristata. *Andros Island, Bahamas.*

Ants, butterflies, and a number of enterprising hummingbirds such as the Puerto Rican Emerald, Western Streamertail, Cuban Emerald, Purple-throated Carib, and Bahama Woodstar take advantage of these "shortcuts" when feeding. And the Purple-crowned Fairy, a South American species, goes one step further by puncturing the flower itself.

The Puerto Rican Emerald robs nectar from the following flowers:

Tabebuia rigida (Bignoniaceae)
Pitcairnia angustifolia (Bromeliaceae)
P. bromeliifolia (Bromeliaceae)
Erythrina berteroana (Papilionaceae [Fabaceae])
Neorudolphia volubilis (Papilionaceae [Fabaceae]).

Both the Puerto Rican Emerald and the Green Mango steal nectar from:

Malvaviscus arboreus (Malvaceae).

And the Cuban Emerald sips nectar from the bases of:

Barleria cristata (Acanthaceae)
Tabebuia rosea (Bignoniaceae).

HUMMINGBIRD MITES

Specialized mites that live out their entire life cycles on certain hummingbird-pollinated wildflowers rely on hummingbirds to transport them from one plant to another. Minute in size—one measures the size of a period on a printed page—they are carried from flower to flower in the nasal passages of the birds as they feed.

When they have reached their destinations, the mites race down the bird's bill at a speed that has been measured and compared, relative to their size, to that of a cheetah.

West Indian hummers seen carrying nasal mites are the Puerto Rican Emerald, Cuban Emerald, Green Mango, Blue-headed Hummingbird, and the Rufous-breasted Hermit. Each was feeding from heliconia flowers when the mites were observed. The bills and nostrils of some Purple-throated Caribs on Martinique were also found to be heavily populated with mites.

Seventeen species of these mites, belonging to three genera, have been identified in the Caribbean. Most common are the eight different species of *Rhinoseius*. The others belong to *Proctolaelaps* or *Lasioseius*. One of these, *Tropicoseius bakeri,* is associated with the Cuban Emerald.

These tiny mites are capable of running at a speed that can be compared, relatively speaking, to that of a cheetah. Rhinoseius hirsuta.

There are certain mites that travel from flower to flower in the nasal passages of hummingbirds. Rhinoscius colwelli.

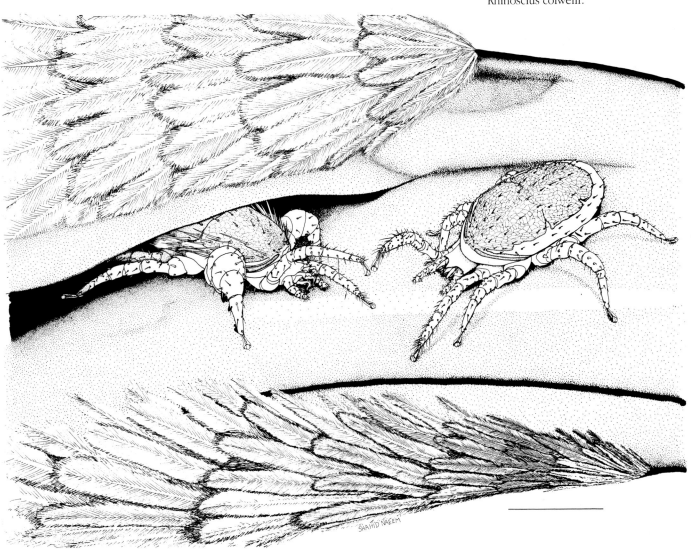

WILDFLOWERS

Throughout the years, scientists and naturalists have been diligent about listing the many flowers from which they have seen hummingbirds feed and pollinate. What follows is a list of these beautiful blossoms.

Note: Information on ranges relates only to the islands of the Caribbean and was gathered from personal observations as well as citations from scientific literature, including both general distribution and local floristic works. It is possible that some floral species may also be found in countries not named on this list.

The symbol * denotes a flower pollinated by hummingbirds. The symbol †, a flower visited by hummingbirds, and the symbol ‡, a flower whose nectar is robbed by hummingbirds.

MONOCOTYLEDONS

AGAVACEAE *Agave braceana*
Century Plant; Brace's Century Plant (Bahamas)
The Bahamas
† Visited by the Cuban Emerald

A. sisalana
Sisal, Sisal Hemp, Hemp Plant; Sisal, Henequén (Cuba)
The Bahamas; Cuba and Jamaica; Greater Antilles; St. Martin, St. Barthélemy, St. Kitts, Nevis,
   Montserrat, Barbados, and Grenada; Lesser Antilles
† Visited in the Bahamas by the Bahama Woodstar

Yucca gloriosa
Spanish Dagger, Palm Lily, Roman Candle, Lord's Candlestick; Bayoneta, Espino (Cuba);
   Salsepareille (French)
West Indies; Cuba and Guadeloupe

BROMELIACEAE *Aechmea* sp.
Dominican Republic
† Visited by the Hispaniolan Emerald

Ananas comosus
Pineapple, Sweet Pine, Ananas, Pine; Piña (Puerto Rico); Piña (Cuba); Ananas Panache
   (French)
Cuba and Jamaica

Guzmania berteroniana
Flaming Torch
Puerto Rico—endemic
* Pollinated by the Green Mango

G. monostachia
Striped Torch; Curujey (Cuba)
West Indies, including Cuba and Jamaica
† Visited in Jamaica by the Streamertail

Hohenbergia penduliflora
Curujey de Paredón (Cuba)
West Indies, including Cuba and Jamaica
† Visited in Jamaica by the Streamertail and the Jamaican Mango

H. portorricensis
Puerto Rico—endemic
* Pollinated by the Puerto Rican Emerald

Pitcairnia angustifolia
Erizo, Pina Cortadora, Pina de Cuervo (Puerto Rico)
Puerto Rico; Lesser Antilles, including Antigua, Saba, St. Eustatius, St. Kitts, Montserrat,
   Guadeloupe, Dominica, Martinique, St. Lucia, St. Vincent, the Grenadines, Barbados, and
   Grenada
† Visited in Puerto Rico by the Green Mango
‡ Puerto Rican Emerald is nectar robber

P. bromeliifolia
West Indies, including Jamaica and Puerto Rico
* Pollinated in Puerto Rico by the Green Mango and the Antillean Mango
† Visited by the Puerto Rican Emerald
‡ Puerto Rican Emerald is nectar robber

Tillandsia utriculata
Ananas Sauvage, Ananas Marron, Wild Pine; Swollen Wild Pine (Bahamas); Curujey (Cuba)
West Indies—Bahamas; Cuba to Anegada; the Lesser Antilles, including Anguilla, St. Martin,
  St. Barthélemy, Antigua, Barbuda, Saba, St. Eustatius, St. Kitts, Nevis, Montserrat,
  Guadeloupe, La Desirade, Dominica, Martinique, St. Lucia, St. Vincent, the Grenadines,
  and Grenada
* Pollinated in Puerto Rico by the Green Mango and the Antillean Mango

Tillandsia sp.
Jamaica
† Visited in Jamaica by the Streamertail
Vriesea ringens
Puerto Rico

V. sintenisii
Greater Antilles, including Cuba, Jamaica, and Puerto Rico; Guadeloupe
* Pollinated in Puerto Rico by the Puerto Rican Emerald
† Visited in Puerto Rico by the Green Mango

CANNACEAE   *Canna indica*
Maraca Roja (Puerto Rico)
Puerto Rico and Jamaica
† Visited in Jamaica by the Streamertail

HELICONIACEAE   *Heliconia bihai*
Lobster's Claw; Wild Plantain, Balisier; Balisier (Martinique)
Jamaica, Martinique
† Visited in the Dominican Republic by the Hispaniolan Emerald
†Visited in Martinique by the Green-throated Carib, the Purple-throated Carib, and the Blue-
    headed Hummingbird
† Visited in Grenada by the Rufous-breasted Hermit

Female Rufous-breasted Hermit/Wild Plantain (Heliconia bihai). *Grand Étang, Grenada.*

Female Rufous-breasted Hermit/Wild Plantain (Heliconia bihai). *Grand Étang, Grenada.*

H. caribaea
Lobster-claws, Wild Plantain, Balisier; Platano Cimarrón (Cuba); Balisier (Martinique)
Greater Antilles; Lesser Antilles, including Antigua, Montserrat, Guadeloupe, Dominica,
    Martinique, St. Lucia, St. Vincent, and Grenada
† Visited in the Dominican Republic by the Hispaniolan Emerald
† Visited in Dominica by the Purple-throated Carib
† Visited in Martinique by the Blue-headed Hummingbird, the Green-throated Carib, and the
    Purple-throated Carib
† Visited in St. Lucia by the Purple-throated Carib

H. collinsiana
Martinique
† Visited by Blue-headed Hummingbird, the Green-throated Carib, and the Purple-throated
    Carib

Female Purple-throated Carib/
Lobster-claws (Heliconia caribaea).
Lamentin, Martinique.

Female Purple-throated Carib/
Heliconia collinsiana. *Lamentin,*
Martinique.

*Male Puerto Rican Emerald/Parrot's
Plantain* (Heliconia psittacorum).
El Yunque, Puerto Rico.

H. psittacorum
Parrot's Plantain, Parrot's Flower, Parakeet; Balisier (Martinique)
Puerto Rico, St. Kitts, Guadeloupe, Martinique, St. Lucia, and Grenada
† Visited in Puerto Rico by the Puerto Rican Emerald and the Antillean Crested Hummingbird
† Visited in Martinique by the Antillean Crested Hummingbird
† Visited in Grenada by the Antillean Crested Hummingbird

H. rostrata
Pendant Firebirds, Hanging Lobster-claws
Jamaica, Martinique, and Grenada
† Visited in Jamaica by the Eastern and Western Streamertails
† Visited in Martinique by the Blue-headed Hummingbird, the Green-throated Carib, and the
   Purple-throated Carib
† Visited in Grenada by the Rufous-breasted Hermit

H. swartziana
Jamaica
† Visited by the Streamertail and the Jamaican Mango

Heliconia sp.
Puerto Rico
† Visited by the Green Mango

LILIACEAE   *Aloe vera*
Aloe, Barbados Aloe, Bitter Aloes, Curaçao Aloe, Sempervivum, Sentebibu, Sinkle Bible
   Jamaica, Medicinal Aloe, Unguentine Cactus; Sábila (Cuba)
Bahamas, Cuba, and the Lesser Antilles, including St. Martin, St. Barthélemy, Antigua,
   Guadeloupe, Dominica, St. Eustatius, Martinique, St. Lucia, St. Vincent, and Barbados;
   Grand Cayman
† Visited in Cuba by the Bee Hummingbird

Hemerocallis fulva
Orange Daylily, Tawny Daylily, Fulvous Daylily; Lirio Turco (Cuba)
Cuba, Jamaica, and the French West Indies

MARANTACEAE   *Thalia geniculata*
Jamaica
† Visited by the Streamertail and the Jamaican Mango

Male Eastern Streamertail/Pendant Firebirds (Heliconia rostrata). *Port Antonio, Jamaica.*

Female Blue-headed Hummingbird/
Bananier d'Ornement (Musa ornata).
Martinique.

Male Jamaican Mango/Bananier
d'Ornement (Musa ornata). *Crystal*
Spring, Jamaica.

MUSACEAE *Musa ornata*
Bananier d'Ornement (Martinique)
Jamaica and Martinique
† Visited in Jamaica by the Jamaican Mango
† Visited in Martinique by the Green-throated Carib, the Purple-throated Carib, and the Blue-
headed Hummingbird

Musa x *paradisiaca*
Edible Banana Plantain; Banano, Guineo (Puerto Rico); Plátano (Cuba)
Cuba, Puerto Rico, and Dominica
* Pollinated in Puerto Rico by the Puerto Rican Emerald, the Green Mango, and the Antillean
Mango
† Visited in Dominica by the Purple-throated Carib

ORCHIDACEAE *Dilomilis montana*
Puerto Rico
* Pollinated by the Puerto Rican Emerald
Epidendrum sp.
Puerto Rico
* Pollinated by the Puerto Rican Emerald

STRELITZIACEAE *Strelitzia reginae*
Bird of Paradise, Bird of Paradise Flower, Queen's Bird of Paradise, Crane Flower, Crane Lily;
Ave del Paraíso (Cuba); Oiseau de Paradis (French)
Cuba

ZINGIBERACEAE *Alpinia purpurata*
Red Ginger; Alpinia Roja (Cuba); Red Ginger, A Tous Maux (Martinique)
Cuba, Dominican Republic, Martinique, and Grenada
† Visited in the Dominican Republic by the Antillean Mango
† Visited in Martinique by the Green-throated Carib and the Antillean Crested Hummingbird
† Visited in Grenada by the Antillean Crested Hummingbird

Female Antillean Crested Hummingbird/Red Ginger (Alpinia purpurata). *Grand Étang, Grenada.*

189

Female Purple-throated Carib/Torch Ginger (Etlingera elatior). *Lamentin, Martinique.*

A. zerumbet
Shellflower, Shell Ginger, Pink Porcelain Lily
Cuba and Martinique

Etlingera elatior
Torch Ginger, Philippine Waxflower; Rose de Porcelaine (Martinique)
Martinique
† Visited by the Green-throated Carib and the Purple-throated Carib

Hedychium coronarium
White Ginger, White Ginger Lily, Garland Flower, Butterfly Ginger, Butterfly Lily, Ginger Lily,
    Cinnamon Jasmine; Jazmín Cimarrón, Jazmín de Río, Mariposa Blanca, Narciso, Nardo,
    Dulce Nieve, Butterfly Lily, Garland Flower, Ginger Lily (Puerto Rico); Canne d'Eau,
    Canne Rivière, Gingembre Douleur; Mariposa (Cuba); Lis de la Vierge, Canne d'Eau,
    Longose (French)
Cuba, Jamaica, Puerto Rico; the Lesser Antilles, including Guadeloupe, Dominica, and St.
    Vincent
* Pollinated in Puerto Rico by the Puerto Rican Emerald
† Visited in Jamaica by the Streamertail

Renealmia antillarum
Gengibre (Puerto Rico); Colonia Cimarrona, Cojate (Cuba)
Greater Antilles, including Cuba and Puerto Rico; Martinique
* Pollinated in Puerto Rico by the Puerto Rican Emerald, the Green Mango, and the Antillean
    Mango

DICOTYLEDONS

ACANTHACEAE   *Asystasia gangetica*
Asistasia (Cuba); Thunbergia Rampant (Martinique)
Cuba, Jamaica, and Martinique
† Visited in Jamaica by the Eastern Streamertail and the Western Streamertail
† Visited in Martinique by the Antillean Crested Hummingbird

Barleria cristata
Blue Bell, Philippine Violet
Jamaica
† Visited by the Streamertail

Crossandra infundibuliformis
Firecracker Flower; Crosandra (Cuba)
Cuba

Dicliptera aff. *assurgens*
The Bahamas
† Visited by the Cuban Emerald

Female Eastern Streamertail/Asystasia gangetica. *Port Antonio, Jamaica.*

Male Cuban Emerald/Barleria cristata. *Andros Island, Bahamas.*

Female Western Streamertail/
Cardinal's Guard (Pachystachys
spicata). *Kingston, Jamaica.*

Goldfussia glomerata
Mexican Petunia
Jamaica
† Visited by the Streamertail

Graptophyllum pictum
Caricature Plant, Match-Me-Not; Papagayo (Cuba); Caricature (Martinique)
Cuba, Jamaica, and Martinique
† Visited in Martinique by the Antillean Crested Hummingbird

Justicia brandegeana
Shrimp Plant, Mexican Shrimp Plant, Shrimp Bush, False Hop; Plante Crevette, Queue
    d'Écrevisse (French)
Jamaica, Dominican Republic, and Puerto Rico

J. martinsoniana
Puerto Rico—endemic
* Pollinated by the Puerto Rican Emerald

Odontonema nitidum
Lesser Antilles

O. tubiforme
Bois Indien, Bois Genou
Cuba and Martinique
† Visited in Martinique by the Antillean Crested Hummingbird

Pachystachys lutea
Lollypops, Super Goldy; Panache d'Officier (French)
Jamaica, Dominican Republic, and Martinique
† Visited in Jamaica by the Vervain Hummingbird
† Visited in the Dominican Republic by the Vervain Hummingbird
† Visited in Martinique by the Antillean Crested Hummingbird

Female Antillean Mango/Sanchezia nobilis. *Santo Domingo, Dominican Republic.*

P. spicata
Cardinal's Guard; Coral (Cuba); Panache d'Officier (French)
West Indies, including Cuba, Jamaica, Martinique, and Grenada
† Visited in Jamaica by the Streamertail
† Visited in Grenada by the Antillean Crested Hummingbird

Ruellia coccinea
Yerba Maravilla (Puerto Rico)
West Indies, including Puerto Rico
* Pollinated in Puerto Rico by the Puerto Rican Emerald

Sanchezia nobilis
Dominican Republic and Puerto Rico
* Pollinated by the Puerto Rican Emerald
† Visited in the Dominican Republic by the Antillean Mango

Thunbergia alata
Black-eyed Susan, Black-eyed Susan Vine; Winged Thunbergia (Bahamas); Ojo de Poeta
    (Cuba); Liane Fleur Violette, Liane de Chine (French)
The Bahamas, Cuba to Tortola and Trinidad
† Visited in Jamaica by the Streamertail

T. erecta
King's Mantle, Bush Clock Vine; Angelina, Boca Vieja, Violeta, Viuda (Puerto Rico); Mainereta
    (Cuba); Gueule de Loup (Martinique)
Cuba, Puerto Rico, and Martinique
* Pollinated in Puerto Rico by the Green Mango
† Visited in Martinique by the Antillean Crested Hummingbird, the Green-throated Carib, and
    the Purple-throated Carib

ANACARDIACEAE   *Anacardium occidentale*
Cashew, Cashew Nut, Cashew Apple; Cajuil, Maranón, Pajuil (Puerto Rico); Cajuil (Dominican
    Republic); Maranon (Cuba); Acajou, Noix d'Acajou, Pomme d'Acajou, Pommier d'Acajou
    (French); Pomme Cajou (Guadeloupe); Cashu, Palu di Cashupete, Kasjoe, Cashew, Cherry
    (Dutch)
West Indies, except the Bahamas
* Pollinated in Puerto Rico by the Puerto Rican Emerald
† Visited in Jamaica by the Vervain Hummingbird

ANNONACEAE   *Annona muricata*
Sour Sop, Prickly Custard Apple; Guanábana (Puerto Rico); Guanábana (Cuba); Guanabana,
    Corossol (Haiti, French West Indies); Sorsaka, Zuurzak Soursap (Dutch West Indies)
West Indies, except the Bahamas

APOCYNACEAE   *Allamanda cathartica*
Yellow Allamanda, Golden Trumpet, Golden Trumpet Bush; Alamanda, Canario, Cautiva
    (Puerto Rico); Alamanda, Flor de Barbero (Cuba); Liane à Lait, Monette Jaune (French)
Cuba, Jamaica, Puerto Rico, and Martinique
† Visited in Martinique by the Antillean Crested Hummingbird

Allamanda sp.
Dominica
† Visited by the Antillean Crested Hummingbird

Nerium oleander
Oleander; Adelfa, Oleander, Alelí, Alhelí, Alelí Extranjero, Laurel Rosado (Puerto Rico); Adelfa,
    Rosa Francesa, Narciso (Cuba); Oleander (Virgin Islands); Martinica, Rosa del Perú, Pirulí
    (Dominican Republic); Laurier Rose, Laurier Tropical (Haiti); Laurier Rose, Oleandre
    (French); Franse Bloem, Oleander (Dutch Antilles)
The Bahamas; Greater Antilles; Virgin Islands; Lesser Antilles

Thevetia peruviana
Trumpet Flower, Yellow Oleander, Lucky Nut, Lucky Nuts, Lucky Seeds, Milk Bush, Be-Still
    Tree; Cabalonga, Lucky Nut, Caballón (Puerto Rico); Cabalonga (Cuba); Lucky Nut (Virgin
    Islands); Retama (Dominican Republic); Luck Seed (West Indies); Luckybean-Bush, Good-
    Luck Tree (Barbados); Bois Saisissement, Serpent, d'Eau Livre (Haiti); Bois-Lait (French);
    Joro-joro, Olijfi di Bonaire, Yellow Oleander (Dutch Antilles)
The Bahamas; Greater Antilles; Virgin Islands; Lesser Antilles

Urechites lutea
Nightsage, Nightshade; Catesby's Vine, Wild Unction (Bahamas); Curamaguey, Bejuco
    Marruyero (Cuba)
The Bahamas; Greater Antilles; Lesser Antilles south to St. Vincent; and the Cayman Islands
† Visited in Jamaica by the Streamertail

ARALIACEAE   *Dendropanax pendulus*
Jamaica
† Visited by the Streamertail

Schefflera sp.
Umbrella Tree, Rubber Tree, Starleaf; Cheflera (Cuba)
Cuba and Jamaica
†Visited in Jamaica by the Streamertail

ASCLEPIADACEAE   *Asclepias curassavica*
Redhead, Red Top, Bloodflower; Wild Ipecac, Hippo (Bahamas); Algodoncillo, Platanillo,
    Yerba de Mariposas, Platanillo Matizado (Puerto Rico); Flor de la Calentura (Cuba);
    Herbe à Ouate, Zebe-papillon, Quadrille, Chapeau Chinois (French)
The Bahamas, Cuba, Jamaica, and Puerto Rico; West Indies
*Pollinated in Puerto Rico by the Puerto Rican Emerald
†Visited in Jamaica by the Streamertail and the Vervain Hummingbird

BALSAMINACEAE   *Impatiens suttonii*
Miramelinda
Puerto Rico
* Pollinated by the Puerto Rican Emerald

BEGONIACEAE   *Begonia coccinea*
Angel-wing; Begonia (Cuba); Begonia, Oseille Bois (Martinique)
Cuba and Martinique

B. manicata
Begonia (Cuba); Begonia, Oseille Bois (French)
Cuba

B. minor
Begonia (Cuba)
Cuba and Martinique

BIGNONIACEAE   *Crescentia cujete*
Calabash, Calabash Tree, Common Calabash Tree; Higuera, Higuero (Puerto Rico); Guira,
    Calabasa (Cuba); Guira, Higuero (Dominican Republic); Calebasse, Calebassier (French);
    Calba's, Calba's Rondo (Dutch West Indies)
The Bahamas, Cuba, Jamaica, Martinique, and Grand Cayman; West Indies

Saritaea magnifica
Saritea (Cuba); Bignone (French)
Cuba, Jamaica, and the Virgin Islands
† Visited in Jamaica by the Streamertail

Spathodea campanulata
Tulip Tree, African Tulip Tree, African Flame Tree, Flame of the Forest; Tulipán Africano,
    African Tuliptree (Puerto Rico); Espatodea (Cuba); Mampolo, Amapola (Dominican
    Republic); Immortel Étranger (Haiti); Tulpenboom (Dutch West Indies)
West Indies, including the Bahamas, Cuba, Jamaica, Haiti, Dominican Republic, Puerto Rico,
    Guadeloupe, Dominica, St. Lucia, and the Dutch West Indies
* Pollinated in Puerto Rico by the Puerto Rican Emerald and the Green Mango
† Visited in Jamaica by the Streamertail and the Jamaican Mango
† Visited in Guadaloupe by the Purple-throated Carib
† Visited in Dominica by the Purple-throated Carib
† Visited in St. Lucia by the Purple-throated Carib and the Green-throated Carib

Tabebuia haemantha
Trumpet Tree
Cuba and Puerto Rico
* Pollinated in Puerto Rico by the Puerto Rican Emerald, the Green Mango, and the Antillean
    Mango

T. rigida
Trumpet Tree; Roble de Sierra (Puerto Rico)
Cuba and Puerto Rico
* Pollinated in Puerto Rico by the Green Mango
† Visited in Puerto Rico by the Puerto Rican Emerald
‡ Puerto Rican Emerald is nectar robber

T. riparia
Trumpet Tree, Pink Trumpet Tree, Whitewood, White Cedar; Roble, Roble Blanco, Roble de
    Yugo, Roble Prieto, Prieto, Roble de Costa, White Cedar (Puerto Rico); Pink Manjack,
    Pink-Cedar, Tooshe-Flower (Virgin Islands); White Cedar (St. Kitts to Grenada); Poirier
    (St. Lucia); Poirier Gris, Poirier Rouge, Poirier Blanc (Guadeloupe, French)
Jamaica, Haiti, Dominican Republic, Puerto Rico, Virgin Islands, and throughout the Lesser
    Antilles
† Visited in Jamaica by the Jamaican Mango
† Visited in Dominica by the Purple-throated Carib

T. rosea
Cuba
† Visited in Cuba by the Cuban Emerald
‡ Cuban Emerald is nectar robber

T. schumanniana
Roble Colorado, Roble de Sierra, Roble Cimarrón
Puerto Rico
* Pollinated by the Puerto Rican Emerald, the Green Mango, and the Antillean Mango

Tecoma stans
Yellowbells, Yellow Elder, Yellow Bignonia, Yellow Trumpet, Florida Yellow Trumpet, Yellow
    Trumpet Flower; Trumpet Flower (Bahamas); Roble Amarillo, Ginger-Thomas, Saúco
    Amarillo, Ruibarba (Puerto Rico); Yellow Elder, Yellow Cedar (Virgin Islands); Saúco

Tabebuia rosea. *Playa Larga,
Ciénega de Zapata, Cuba.*

Amarillo (Dominican Republic, Cuba); Coribee (Antigua); Bois Caraibe (Grenada); Chevalier (Haiti); Bois Fleurs Jaunes; Bois-Pissenlit (Guadeloupe, St. Lucia); Kelki Heel, Yellow-Blossom (Dutch West Indies)
West Indies, including the Bahamas, Jamaica, and Grand Cayman
† Visited in Jamaica by the Streamertail

Tecomaria capensis
Cape Honeysuckle; Jazmín Trompeta (Cuba); Jasmin Trompette, Chèvre-Feuille du Cap (Martinique)
The Bahamas, Cuba, Jamaica, and Martinique
† Visited in the Bahamas by the Bahama Woodstar

BORAGINACEAE   *Bourreria baccata*
Jamaica
† Visited by the Vervain Hummingbird

B. venosa
Jamaica and the Cayman Islands
† Visited in Jamaica by the Vervain Hummingbird

Cordia collococca
Clammy Cherry; Palo de Muñeca, Manjack, Cerezo (Puerto Rico); Muñeco, Palo de Muñeco Blanco (Dominican Republic); Ateje, Ateje Hembra (Cuba); Cherry, Wild Cherry (Jamaica); Clammy-Cherry (Grenada); Clammy Cherry, Wild Clammy Cherry (Barbados); Mapou (St. Barthélemy, Guadeloupe); Mapou Blanc, Mahot Rivière (Martinique); Trois Pieds (Haiti)
Greater Antilles, including Cuba, Jamaica, Haiti, Dominican Republic, and Puerto Rico; Lesser Antilles, including Vieques, St. Barthélemy, Guadeloupe, Martinique, Barbados, and Grenada
* Pollinated in Puerto Rico by the Puerto Rican Emerald
† Visited in Puerto Rico by the Antillean Crested Hummingbird
† Visited in Vieques by the Antillean Crested Hummingbird

C. gerascanthus
Panchallon, Spanish Elm; Baría, Varía, Varía Prieta (Cuba)
Greater Antilles; Cayman Islands
† Visited in Jamaica by the Streamertail

C. globosa
Rough Varronia, Cocobey (Bahamas); Hierba de la Sangre (Cuba)
The Bahamas, Cuba, and Jamaica
† Visited in Jamaica by the Vervain Hummingbird

C. rickseckeri
San Bartolomé, Manjack, Lija (Puerto Rico); Dog Almond, Black Manjack (Tortola)
Puerto Rico, Vieques, Culebra, St. Thomas, and Tortola
* Pollinated in Puerto Rico by the Green Mango and the Antillean Mango

C. sebestena
Anaconda, Geiger Tree, Red or Scarlet Cordia; Spanish Cordia (Bahamas); Vomitel Colorado,
Geiger Tree, Anaconda, Cereza Amarilla (Puerto Rico); Avellano Criollo (Dominican
Republic); Vomitel Colorado, Anacaguita (Cuba); Scarlet Cordia (Barbados); Red Cordia,
Scarlet Cordia (Jamaica); Coquelicot, Petit Soleil (Haiti); Mapou Rouge, Sebestier
(French); Scarlet Accordia, Scarlet Flower, Cawara Spano, Manhage (Dutch Antilles)
West Indies, including the Bahamas, Cuba, Jamaica, Puerto Rico, the Virgin Islands, and Grand
Cayman
† Visited in Jamaica by the Streamertail and the Jamaican Mango

CACTACEAE *Lemaireocereus hystrix*
Dildo, Dildo Pear; Dildo Español (Puerto Rico); Cardón (Cuba)
West Indies
† Visited in Jamaica by the Jamaican Mango and the Vervain Hummingbird

Melocactus communis
Turk's Cap, Turk's Head, Melon Cactus
The Bahamas and Jamaica
† Visited in Jamaica by the Streamertail

M. intortus
Turk's Cap; Melón de Costa (Puerto Rico)
Puerto Rico
* Pollinated by the Puerto Rican Emerald and the Antillean Mango

Melocactus sp.
St. Lucia
† Visited by the Purple-throated Carib

Opuntia dillenii
Prickly Pear, Seaside Tuna; Common Prickly Pear (Bahamas); Tuna, Tuna Brava (Cuba)
West Indies, including the Bahamas, Cuba, Jamaica, Puerto Rico, and Grand Cayman
† Visited in Jamaica by the Jamaican Mango

O. spinosissima
Prickly Pear Tree
Jamaica
† Visited by the Streamertail, the Jamaican Mango, and the Vervain Hummingbird

Opuntia sp.
St. Lucia
† Visited by the Purple-throated Carib

CAESALPINIACEAE *Bauhinia blakeana*
Hong Kong Orchid, Orchid Tree; Arbre Orchidée, Orchidée du Pauvre (Martinique)
Jamaica and Martinique
† Visited in Jamaica by the Jamaican Mango

B. divaricata
Bull Hoof, Moco John; Pata de Vaca (Cuba)
Greater Antilles, including Cuba and Jamaica; St. Kitts; Grand Cayman
† Visited in Jamaica by the Streamertail, the Jamaican Mango and the Vervain Hummingbird

B. monandra
Butterfly Bauhinia, Butterfly Flower, Pink Bauhinia, Pink Orchidtree; Jerusalem Date, Butterfly
Flower (Jamaica); Mariposa, Butterfly Bauhinia, Flamboyán Blanco, Seplina, Varital
Variable, Alas de Ángel, Baujinia (Puerto Rico); Napoleon's Plume, Poor Man's Orchid,
Bauhinia (Virgin Islands); Flamboyán Extranjero, Flamboyán Cubano, Pata de Vaca
(Dominican Republic); Orquídea Silvestre, Casco de Mulo, Casco de Vaca, Pata de Mulo,
Pata de Vaca (Cuba); Deux Jumelles, Caractère des Hommes (Haiti); Arbre Orchidée,
Orchidée du Pauvre (French); Vlinderbloem (Dutch West Indies)
West Indies from Cuba and Jamaica southward
* Pollinated in Puerto Rico by the Puerto Rican Emerald and the Green Mango

Male Jamaican Mango/Orchid Tree (Bauhinia variegata). *Crystal Spring, Jamaica.*

B. variegata
Orchid Tree, Mountain Ebony; Buddhist Bauhinia, Poor Man's Orchid, Palo de Orquídeas
    (Puerto Rico); Bauinia, Orquídea Silvestre (Cuba); Arbre Orchidée, Orchidée du Pauvre
    (French)
Cuba, Jamaica, Puerto Rico, and Martinique
† Visited in Jamaica by the Jamaican Mango
† Visited in Martinique by the Green-throated Carib

Caesalpinia decapetala
Wait-a-Bit
Jamaica
† Visited by the Streamertail

C. pulcherrima
Barbados Pride, Pride of Barbados, Flower Fence, Barbados Flower Fence, Dwarf Poinciana;
    Clavellina (Puerto Rico); Guacamaya (Cuba); Petit Flamboyant, Poinciana, Doudou,
    Orgueil de Chine (French)
West Indies, including the Bahamas, and from Cuba to St. Thomas and Trinidad
† Visited in Jamaica by the Streamertail and the Vervain Hummingbird
† Visited in the Dominican Republic by the Hispaniolan Emerald
† Visited in Puerto Rico by the Antillean Crested Hummingbird
† Visited in Martinique by the Antillean Crested Hummingbird

Cassia sp.
Senna, Shower Tree
Jamaica, Puerto Rico, and Martinique
† Visited in Puerto Rico by the Antillean Crested Hummingbird
† Visited in Martinique by the Antillean Crested Hummingbird

Delonix regia
Poinciana, Royal Poinciana, Flamboyant, Peacock Flower, Mohur Tree; Flamboyán, Flamboyán
    Rojo, Flamboyán Colorado, Flamboyant Tree (Puerto Rico); Flamboyant, Giant, Giant-
    Tree (Virgin Islands); Flamboyán (Dominican Republic); Framboyán, Flamboyant (Cuba);
    Flamboyant (French); Flamboyant, July-Tree (Dutch West Indies)
West Indies, including the Bahamas, Cuba, Jamaica, Dominican Republic, Puerto Rico, Virgin
    Islands, Martinique, Grenada, and the Dutch West Indies
* Pollinated in Puerto Rico by the Puerto Rican Emerald
† Visited in Cuba by the Cuban Emerald
† Visited in Jamaica by the Vervain Hummingbird
† Visited in Puerto Rico by the Antillean Mango and the Antillean Crested Hummingbird
† Visited in Martinique by the Green-throated Carib, the Purple-throated Carib, and the
    Antillean Crested Hummingbird
† Visited in Grenada by the Antillean Crested Hummingbird

Tamarindus indica
Tamarindo (Cuba); Taman, Tamarindade (Virgin Islands); Tamarin, Tamarinier, Tamarindier
  (French); Tamarijn, Tamarind (Dutch West Indies)
West Indies, including the Bahamas, Cuba, Jamaica, and the Dutch West Indies
† Visited in Jamaica by the Vervain Hummingbird

CAMPANULACEAE   *Platycodon grandiflorus*
Balloon Flower
Jamaica

CARICACEAE   *Carica papaya*
Papaya, Papaw, Pawpaw, Melon Tree; Lechosa, Papaya (Puerto Rico); Papay, Pawpaw (Virgin
  Islands); Fruta Bomba, Papaya (Cuba); Papaye, Papayer (French); Papaya, Papao, Papay
  (Dutch West Indies)
West Indies, including the Bahamas, Cuba, Puerto Rico, the Virgin Islands, Martinique, and the
  Dutch West Indies

CHRYSOBALANACEAE   *Hirtella rugosa*
Coco Plum, Icaquillo, Hicaquillo, Jicaquillo, Juanilla, Teta de Burra Cimarrona (Puerto Rico);
  Hicaco (Cuba)
Cuba and Puerto Rico
* Pollinated in Puerto Rico by the Puerto Rican Emerald

CLETHRACEAE   *Clethra occidentalis*
Soapwood White Alder, Summer Sweet
Jamaica
† Visited by the Streamertail

COMBRETACEAE   *Combretum fruticosum*
Burning Bush
Martinique
† Visited in Martinique by the Green-throated Carib and the Purple-throated Carib

Laguncularia racemosa
White Mangrove, White Buttonwood; White Mangrove, Bastard Buttonwood, Green Turtle
  Bush, Green Turtle-bough (Bahamas); Mangle Blanco, Mangle Bobo (Puerto Rico);
  Mangel (Virgin Islands); Mangle Amarillo, Mangle Prieto (Dominican Republic); Patabán
  (Cuba); Mangle, Manglier Blanc (Haiti); Palétuvier (French); Mangle Blanc, Manglier
  Blanc (Guadeloupe)
West Indies except Dominica
† Visited in Cuba by the Bee Hummingbird
† Visited in Jamaica by the Vervain Hummingbird

Quisqualis indica
Rangoon Creeper; Cocuisa, Corazón de Hombre (Puerto Rico); Piscuala (Cuba); Caractère des
  Hommes, Liseron des Indes (French)
Cuba, Jamaica, and Puerto Rico
† Visited in Puerto Rico by the Green Mango

COMPOSITAE   *Ageratum* sp.
(ASTERACEAE)   Flossflower, Pussy-foot; Mentastro, Yerba de Cabrío (Puerto Rico)
West Indies
† Visited in Jamaica by the Vervain Hummingbird

Clibadium erosum
Carruzo, Turmá de Oro (Puerto Rico)
Puerto Rico
* Pollinated by the Puerto Rican Emerald

Piptocarpha tetrantha
Puerto Rico—endemic
* Pollinated by the Puerto Rican Emerald

CONVOLVULACEAE   *Ipomoea arenaria*
Morning Glory; Cambustera (Cuba)
Cuba and Puerto Rico
* Pollinated in Puerto Rico by the Green Mango and the Antillean Mango

I. repanda
Puerto Rico—endemic
* Pollinated by the Puerto Rican Emerald, Green Mango, and the Antillean Mango

Ipomoea sp.
Trumpet Creeper
Jamaica and Puerto Rico
† Visited in Jamaica by the Streamertail
† Visited in Puerto Rico by the Green Mango

COSTACEAE   *Costus speciosus*
Crepe Ginger, Spiral Ginger, Wild Ginger; Costus (Cuba); Canne d'Eau (French)
Greater Antilles, including Cuba and Jamaica; Lesser Antilles, including St. Eustatius,
    Guadeloupe, Martinique, St. Lucia, St. Vincent, and Grenada

CRASSULACEAE   *Kalanchoe* sp.
Palm Beach Bells; Prodigiosa, Flor de Aire (Cuba)
Cuba and the U.S. Virgin Islands
† Visited in the U.S. Virgin Islands by the Green-throated Carib

ERICACEAE   *Vaccinium meridionale*
Bilberry
Jamaica
† Visited by the Streamertail and the Vervain Hummingbird

EUPHORBIACEAE   *Acalypha hispida*
Chenille, Queue de Chat, Jupon-cancan, Cancan, Foulard
Martinique
† Visited in Martinique by the Green-throated Carib and the Purple-throated Carib

A. wilkesiana
Heart Copperleaf; Acalifa, Capa de Obispo, Primavera (Puerto Rico); Chenille, Queue de Chat,
    Jupon-cancan, Cancan, Foulard (French)
Puerto Rico
* Pollinated by the Puerto Rican Emerald

Croton linearis
Rosemary; Linear-leaved Croton, Bay Wormwood, Granny Bush (Bahamas)
The Bahamas, Jamaica, Haiti, Dominican Republic, and Grand Cayman
† Visited in Jamaica by the Vervain Hummingbird

Euphorbia sp.
Jamaica, Puerto Rico, and U.S. Virgin Islands
† Visited in Puerto Rico by the Antillean Crested Hummingbird
† Visited in the U.S. Virgin Islands by the Green-throated Carib and the Antillean Crested
    Hummingbird

Pedilanthus tithymaloides
Monkey Fiddle, Japanese Poinsettia, Redbird Flower, Redbird Cactus, Ribbon Cactus, Slipper
    Flower, Slipper Plant, Jewbush, Devil's Backbone; Fiddle Flower (Bahamas); Bejuco de
    Estrella (Puerto Rico); Itamo Real, Zapatico (Cuba); Herbe à Cors, Boit Lait, Grosses
    Oreilles, Pantoufle (French)
West Indies, including the Bahamas, Cuba, and Jamaica
† Visited in Jamaica by the Streamertail

GENTIANACEAE   *Lisianthius laxiflorus*
Campanilla Amarilla (Puerto Rico)
West Indies, including Puerto Rico
* Pollinated in Puerto Rico by the Puerto Rican Emerald

GESNERIACEAE   *Alloplectus cristatus*
Fuchsia, Crête à Coq (French)
Lesser Antilles, including Martinique

Besleria lanceolata
Martinique, the Lesser Antilles

B. lutea
Cuba, Jamaica, Haiti, Dominican Republic, and the rainier islands of the Lesser Antilles
† Visited in Jamaica by the Streamertail

Male Antillean Crested
Hummingbird/Kohlaria tubiflora.
Grand Étang, Grenada.

Chrysothemis pulchella
Herbe à Miel (French)
West Indies

Columnea hirsuta
Jamaica—endemic
† Visited by the Streamertail

Episcia cupreata
Carpet Plant, Flame Violet; Episcia (Cuba); Culotte du Diable (French)
Cuba

Gesneria pedunculosa
Arbol de Navidad
Puerto Rico—endemic
* Pollinated by the Puerto Rican Emerald

Kohlaria tubiflora
Grenada
† Visited by the Antillean Crested Hummingbird

Nautilocalyx melittifolius
Lesser Antilles, including Martinique

Rhytidophyllum auriculatum
Dominican Republic
† Visited by the Hispaniolan Emerald

GUTTIFERAE *Clusia krugiana*
Cupeíllo (Puerto Rico)
Puerto Rico
* Pollinated by the Puerto Rican Emerald

C. minor
Cupey Trepador (Puerto Rico)
Puerto Rico
* Pollinated by the Puerto Rican Emerald

LABIATAE *Leonotis nepetifolia*
(LAMIACEAE) Lion's Ear, Bald Bush, Christmas Candlestick; Botón de Cadete, Molinillo, Quinino del Pasto
(Puerto Rico); Varita de San José, Bastón de San Francisco, Molinillo (Cuba)
West Indies, including Cuba, Jamaica, Puerto Rico, and Vieques
† Visited in Jamaica by the Streamertail and the Jamaican Mango
† Visited in Vieques by the Antillean Mango

Plectranthus blumei
Joseph's Coat; Coleo, Nazareno, Tocador, Vergüenza, Coleus (Puerto Rico); Robe à l'Évêque,
    Tapis Monseigneur, Vieux Garçon (French)
Jamaica and Puerto Rico
* Pollinated in Puerto Rico by the Puerto Rican Emerald
† Visited in Jamaica by the Vervain Hummingbird

P. nummularius
Swedish Ivy
Martinique

Salvia sp.
Sage, Ramona; Banderilla (Cuba)
Cuba and Jamaica

LAURACEAE   *Persea* sp.
Martinique

LECYTHIDACEAE   *Couroupita guianensis*
Cannonball Tree; Bala de Canón, Cannonball Tree (Puerto Rico); Bala de Canón (Cuba); Muco
    (Dominican Republic); Boulet de Canon, Arbre à Bombes, Abricot de Singe (French)
West Indies, including Cuba, Dominican Republic, Puerto Rico, and Martinique
† Visited in Martinique by the Antillean Crested Hummingbird

LOBELIACEAE   *Lobelia martagon*
Jamaica
† Visited by the Streamertail
L. portorricensis
Tibey Tupa
Puerto Rico—endemic
* Pollinated by the Puerto Rican Emerald

LORANTHACEAE   *Psittacanthus martinicensis*
Dominica
† Visited by the Purple-throated Carib

LYTHRACEAE   *Cuphea ignea*
Cigar Flower, Firecracker Plant, Red-White-and-Blue Flower
Jamaica
† Visited by the Vervain Hummingbird

Lagerstroemia indica
Crape Myrtle, Common Crapemyrtle, June Rose, Astromelia; Astromelia, Crapemyrtle,
    Stromelia, Astromero, Queen-of-Flowers (Puerto Rico); Júpiter, Astronomía (Cuba);
    Almira, Astromera (Dominican Republic); Stragornia (Haiti); Queen-of-Cribflower,
    Queen-of-the-Garden, Queen-of-Flowers (Dutch Antilles)
Greater Antilles; the Dutch Antilles

L. speciosa
Queen's Crape-Myrtle, Giant Crape Myrtle, Pride of India, Rose of India; Gestrame, Lagerose
    (French)
Puerto Rico
* Pollinated by the Puerto Rican Emerald

MALVACEAE   *Goethea strictiflora*
Martinique

Hibiscus elatus
Blue Mahoe, Cuba Bark, Cuban Bast, Mahoe, Mountain Mahoe; Majó, Mahoe, Emajagua Excelsa
    (Puerto Rico); Majagua, Majagua Azul (Cuba); Mahot Bois Bleu (French)
Greater Antilles; Dominica and Martinique
† Visited in Cuba by the Bee Hummingbird
† Visited in Jamaica by the Streamertail
† Visited in Dominica by the Purple-throated Carib

Male Bahama Woodstar/Hibiscus (Hibiscus rosa-sinensis). *Nassau, Bahamas.*

H. rosa-sinensis
Hibiscus, Chinese Hibiscus, Hawaiian Hibiscus, Rose of China, China Rose, Chinese Rose, Amapola, Shoe Black, Blacking Plant; Amapola, Pavón, Candelá, Candelada, Carta Abierta, Marimona, Hibisco (Puerto Rico); Mar Pacífico (Cuba); Chinese Rose (Virgin Islands); Sangre de Cristo, Cayena (Dominican Republic); Shoe Black (Jamaica, Haiti); Hibiscus, Rose de Chine (French); Hibisc, Cayena, Cayena Dobbel (Dutch Antilles)
Greater Antilles; U.S. Virgin Islands; Martinique, and the Dutch Antilles
* Pollinated in Puerto Rico by the Puerto Rican Emerald and the Green Mango
† Visited in the Bahamas by the Bahama Woodstar
† Visited in the U.S. Virgin Islands by the Antillean Crested Hummingbird
† Visited in the Dominican Republic by the Antillean Mango
† Visited in Martinique by the Green-throated Carib and the Purple-throated Carib

H. schizopetalus
Japanese Hibiscus, Japanese Lantern; Lira (Puerto Rico); Farolito Chino (Cuba); Rose de Chine (Martinique)
Cuba, Dominican Republic, Puerto Rico, U.S. Virgin Islands, and Martinique
† Visited in the Dominican Republic by the Antillean Mango and the Vervain Hummingbird
† Visited in the U.S. Virgin Islands by the Antillean Crested Hummingbird
† Visited in Martinique by the Green-throated Carib and the Purple-throated Carib

H. tiliaceus
Sea Hibiscus, Linden Hibiscus, Tree Hibiscus, Mahoe; Mahoe, Seaside Mahoe, Seaside Majoe (Jamaica); Emajagua, Sea Hibiscus, Majagua (Puerto Rico); Damajagua (Dominican Republic); Majagua, Majagua Hembra (Cuba); Mahot (St. Vincent); Coton Marron, Mahaut Franc (Haiti); Bois Flot, Bois de Liège, Grand Mahot, Mahot Gombo (Guadeloupe); Bois Flot (Martinique)
Greater Antilles; Guadeloupe, Martinique, and St. Vincent
† Visited in Cuba by the Bee Hummingbird
† Visited in Puerto Rico by the Green Mango and the Antillean Mango
† Visited in Martinique by the Green-throated Carib and the Antillean Crested Hummingbird

Hibiscus sp.
Mallow, Rose Mallow, Giant Mallow
Puerto Rico and Dominica
† Visited in Puerto Rico by the Antillean Crested Hummingbird
† Visited in Dominica by the Purple-throated Carib

Malvaviscus arboreus
Mahoe Rose, Sugar Bark, Turk's Cap, Turk's Cup, Wax Mallow; Capucha de Monje (Puerto Rico); Majaguilla (Cuba); Hibiscus Piment, Hibiscus Dormant (Martinique)
West Indies, including Cuba, Jamaica, Dominican Republic, Puerto Rico, Martinique, and Grenada
† Visited in Cuba by the Bee Hummingbird
† Visited in Jamaica by the Streamertail
† Visited in the Dominican Republic by the Hispaniolan Emerald and the Vervain Hummingbird
† Visited in Puerto Rico by the Puerto Rican Emerald and the Green Mango
† Visited in Martinique by the Antillean Crested Hummingbird, the Purple-throated Carib, and the Green-throated Carib
‡‡ Puerto Rican Emerald and the Green Mango are nectar robbers

M. arboreus var. *penduliflorus*
Pepper Hibiscus, Sleeping Hibiscus
Jamaica
† Visited by the Streamertail
Urena lobata
Ballard Bush, Bur Mallow; Cadillo, Cadillo Pata de Perro (Puerto Rico)
Jamaica and Puerto Rico
† Visited in Jamaica by the Streamertail

MARCGRAVIACEAE   *Marcgravia brownei*
Shingle Plant
Jamaica
† Visited by the Streamertail, the Jamaican Mango, and the Vervain Hummingbird

M. rectiflora
Bejuco de Lira, Bejuco de Palma, Pega Palma (Puerto Rico)
Puerto Rico
* Pollinated by the Puerto Rican Emerald

M. sintenisii
Puerto Rico
* Pollinated by the Puerto Rican Emerald

MELASTOMATACEAE   *Heterotrichum cymosum*
Camasey Colorado, Camasey de Paloma, Camasey Terciopelo, Terciopelo (Puerto Rico)
Puerto Rico
* Pollinated by the Puerto Rican Emerald

Mecranium amygdalinum
Camasey Almendro (Puerto Rico)
Puerto Rico
* Pollinated by the Puerto Rican Emerald

Meriania leucantha
Cordobán (Cuba)
Cuba and Jamaica
† Visited in Jamaica by the Streamertail

Miconia quadrangularis
Jamaica
† Visited by the Streamertail and the Vervain Hummingbird

Miconia sp.
Camasey (Puerto Rico)
Puerto Rico
* Pollinated by the Puerto Rican Emerald

MIMOSACEAE   *Acacia farnesiana*
Sweet Acacia, Cassie, Huisache; Rallo, Aroma, Sweet Acacia (Puerto Rico); Casha, Cassia (Virgin
   Islands); Cambrón (Dominican Republic); Aroma, Aroma Amarilla (Cuba); Aroma, Cashia,
   Opoponax (Bahamas); Cassie-Flower (Jamaica); Casha, Cassie (St. Barthélemy); Acacia
   Odorant (Guadeloupe); Casha (Dutch West Indies)
West Indies, including the Bahamas, Cuba, Jamaica, Dominican Republic, Puerto Rico,
   Vieques, Virgin Islands, St. Barthélemy, Guadeloupe, and the Dutch West Indies
† Visited in the Virgin Islands by the Antillean Crested Hummingbird

Acacia sp.
Jamaica
† Visited by the Vervain Hummingbird

Calliandra haematocephala
Pink Powder Puff, Red Powder Puff; Caliandra (Cuba); Pompon Rose, Pompon de Marin
   (French)
Cuba and Martinique

C. pilosa
Powder Puff
Jamaica
† Visited by the Vervain Hummingbird

C. surinamensis
Surinam Calliandra; Caliandra Surinamense (Cuba); Canasta Mexicana (Dominican Republic);
   Pompon Rose, Pompon de Marin (Martinique)

Male Bee Hummingbird/Leucaena leucocephala. *Playa Larga, Ciénega de Zapata, Cuba.*

Cuba, Dominican Republic, and Martinique
† Visited in Martinique by the Blue-headed Hummingbird, the Green-throated Carib, the
    Purple-throated Carib, and the Antillean Crested Hummingbird

Calliandra sp.
Powder Puff
Jamaica
† Visited by the Streamertail and the Jamaican Mango

Inga vera
Panchock, River Koko; Guaba, Guaba del País, Guaba Nativa (Puerto Rico); Guama
    (Dominican Republic); Inga, Guaba (Cuba); Pois Doux, Pois Sucrin, Sucrier, Sucrin
    (Haiti); Pois Doux, Pois Doux Poilu (Guadeloupe); Pois Doux à Paille (Guadeloupe,
    Martinique)
Greater Antilles; Lesser Antilles, including Guadeloupe, Dominica, and Martinique
* Pollinated in Puerto Rico by the Puerto Rican Emerald
† Visited in Haiti by the Antillean Mango
† Visited in Dominica by the Purple-throated Carib

Leucaena leucocephala
Cuba
† Visited by the Bee Hummingbird

MORACEAE   *Cecropia peltata*
Snake Wood, Trumpet Tree, Trumpet-wood, Pumpwood, Shield-shaped Trumpet Tree;
    Yagrumbo Hembra, Yagrumo, Llagrumo, Yagrumo Hembra (Puerto Rico); Yagruma,
    Yagruma Hembra (Cuba); Trumpet-wood (Virgin Islands); Yagrumo, Yagrumo Hembra
    (Dominican Republic); Bois Trompette (Haiti, Guadeloupe); Bois Canon (Guadeloupe,
    Martinique); Wild Papaw (Dutch West Indies)
West Indies from Cuba and Jamaica southward
† Visited in Jamaica by the Streamertail and the Jamaican Mango

MORINGACEAE   *Moringa pterygosperma*
Horse Radish Tree, Drumstick Tree, Ben Nut Tree; Resedá, Ben, Ángela, Jazmín Francés
    (Puerto Rico); Paraíso Francés, Palo Jeringa, Ben (Cuba); Moringa, Palo de Abejas,
    Libertad (Dominican Republic); Benzolivier, Ben Oleifère (Haiti); Maloko (Guadeloupe);
    Benboom, Salaster, Orengga, Moriengo, Brenolli, Orselli (Dutch West Indies)
The Bahamas; Greater Antilles; Guadeloupe and the Dutch West Indies

MYRTACEAE   *Callistemon citrinus*
Bottlebrush, Red Bottlebrush, Crimson Bottle Brush, Lemon Bottlebrush, Citrus-leaf
    Bottlebrush; Limpia Botella (Dominican Republic)
Dominican Republic

Callistemon speciosus
Bottle Brush; Arbre Ecouvillon, Rince-Bouteille (French)
Cuba
† Visited in Cuba by the Cuban Emerald

Eucalyptus sp.
Eucalypt, Australian Gum, Gum Tree, Ironbark, Stringybark
Jamaica
† Visited by the Streamertail

Syzygium jambos
Rose Apple, Malabar Plum; Pomarrosa, Rose-Apple (Puerto Rico); Plum Rose (Virgin Islands);
    Pomo (Dominican Republic); Pomarrosa, Manzana Rosa (Cuba); Pomme d'Eau, Pomme
    Rose, Pommier Rose (French); Plum Rose (Dutch West Indies)
Cuba, Jamaica, Dominican Republic, Puerto Rico, Virgin Islands, Martinique, and the Dutch
    West Indies
* Pollinated in Puerto Rico by the Puerto Rican Emerald and the Green Mango
† Visited in Jamaica by the Streamertail and the Jamaican Mango

S. malaccense
Otaheite Apple, Malay Apple, Ohia, Rose Apple, Large-fruited Rose Apple, Pomerac Jambos;
    Manzana Malaya, Malay Apple, Pomarrosa Malaya, Ohia (Puerto Rico); Cajuilito Sulimán
    (Dominican Republic); Pomarrosa de Malaca, Pera, Pera de Malaca (Cuba); Jamelac,
    Pomme d'Eau, Pomme Rose (French); Pomme de Tahiti, Pomme de Malaisie
    (Guadeloupe)
West Indies, including Cuba, Jamaica, Dominican Republic, Puerto Rico, Guadeloupe, and
    Martinique
* Pollinated in Puerto Rico by the Puerto Rican Emerald and the Green Mango
† Visited in Jamaica by the Streamertail and the Jamaican Mango

NYCTAGINACEAE   *Bougainvillea* sp.
Bougainvillea; Bouganvil, Flor de Papel (Cuba); Bougainville (French)
Cuba, Jamaica, and Martinique
† Visited in Martinique by the Antillean Crested Hummingbird

OLEACEAE   *Jasminum* sp.
Jasmine, Jessamine; Jazmín (Cuba)
Cuba and Jamaica

PAPILIONACEAE   *Cajanus cajan*
(FABACEAE)
Cajan, Catjang, Catjang Pea, Gungo Pea, Pigeon Pea, Congo Pea, Angola Pea, No-Eye Pea, Red
    Gram, Dahl; Gandul (Cuba)
The Bahamas, Cuba, Jamaica, Puerto Rico, Vieques, and the Virgin Islands
† Visited in Puerto Rico by the Green-throated Carib and the Antillean Crested Hummingbird
† Visited in Vieques by the Green-throated Carib and the Antillean Crested Hummingbird
† Visited in the Virgin Islands by the Green-throated Carib and the Antillean Crested
    Hummingbird

Canavalia altipendula
Wild Overlook Bean
Jamaica
† Visited by the Streamertail

C. maritima
Seaside Bean; Mate de Costa (Cuba)
Cuba and Jamaica
† Visited in Jamaica by the Streamertail and the Jamaican Mango

Centrosema plumieri
Butterfly Pea, Conchita, Fee-fee; Flor de Conchitas (Puerto Rico); Conchita (Cuba)
Cuba, Jamaica, and Puerto Rico
† Visited in Jamaica by the Streamertail

Crotalaria falcata
Rattlebox
Jamaica, Haiti, Dominican Republic, Puerto Rico, Dominica, St. Lucia, and Grenada
† Visited in Jamaica by the Streamertail and the Vervain Hummingbird

C. verrucosa
Blue Rattleweed; Purple Rattlebox (Bahamas); Cascabelillo (Cuba)
The Bahamas, Cuba, Jamaica, St. Thomas to Virgin Gorda, Barbados, and Cayman Island
† Visited in Jamaica by the Streamertail

Erythrina berteroana
Coral Tree, Coralbean; Bucare Enano, Bucayo, Bucayo Enano, Bucayo sin Espinas, Machete,
    Machette (Puerto Rico); Machete (Virgin Islands); Pinón (Dominican Republic); Pinón de
    Pito, Pinón de Cerca, Búcare (Cuba); Brucal (Haiti); Griffe du Tigre (French)
Cuba, Haiti, Dominican Republic, Puerto Rico, Virgin Islands, and Martinique
* Pollinated in Puerto Rico by the Green Mango
‡ Puerto Rican Emerald is nectar robber

E. poeppigiana
Mountain Immortelle; Bucayo (Puerto Rico); Pinón, Búcare (Cuba); Griffe du Tigre (French)
Cuba, Puerto Rico, and Grenada
† Visited in Grenada by the Rufous-breasted Hermit

Erythrina sp.
Jamaica
† Visited by the Streamertail and the Jamaican Mango

Gliricidia sepium
Aaron's Rod, Grow Stick, St. Vincent Plum, Quick Stick, Cocoa Shade; Mataratón, Madre de
    Cacao, Mother-of-Cocoa (Puerto Rico); Pea Tree (Virgin Islands); Pinón de Cuba
    (Dominican Republic); Amoroso, Pinón Amoroso, Arbol Florido, Pinón Florido, Bien
    Vestido, Pinón Violento (Cuba); Lilas Étranger (Haiti); Gliricidia (Guadeloupe); Yerba di
    Tonka, Mataratón, Ratonera (Dutch West Indies)
Cuba and Jamaica to the Lesser Antilles
† Visited in Jamaica by the Streamertail

Mucuna sloanei
Horse-eye Bean; Ojo de Caballo (Cuba)
Cuba and Jamaica
† Visited in Jamaica by the Streamertail

Neorudolphia volubilis
Puerto Rico
* Pollinated by the Green Mango and the Antillean Mango
† Visited by the Puerto Rican Emerald
‡ Puerto Rican Emerald is nectar robber

Sabinea punicea
Puerto Rico
* Pollinated by the Puerto Rican Emerald, Green Mango, and the Antillean Mango

Sesbania grandiflora
Agati, Agati Sesbania, Australian Corkwood Tree, Baby Boots, Red Wistaria, Scarlet Wistaria
    Tree, Vegetable Hummingbird; Báculo, Agati, Gallito, Cresta de Gallo (Puerto Rico); Jack-
    in-the-Beanstalk (Virgin Islands); Gallito (Dominican Republic); Cresta de Gallo, Gallito
    Blanco, Gallito Colorado, Zapatón Blanco, Zapatón Rojo, Paloma (Cuba); Agati, Flamingo-
    bill (Bahamas); Pois Vallier (Haiti); Colibri Végétal, Papillon, Fleur-papillon
    (Guadeloupe); Tiger-tongue (Dutch West Indies)
West Indies from Bahamas and Cuba to St. Vincent

Strongylodon macrobotrys
Jade Vine, Philippine Jade Vine; Liane de Jade (French)
Jamaica and Martinique
† Visited in Jamaica by the Jamaican Mango

Male Bee Hummingbird/Scarlet Bush
(Hamelia patens). *Los Ávalos,*
Ciénega de Zapata, Cuba.

PASSIFLORACEAE   *Passiflora lancifolia*
Passionflower
Jamaica
† Visited by the Streamertail

PITTOSPORACEAE   *Pittosporum undulatum*
Mock Orange, Sweet Pittosporum; Pitosporum (Cuba)
Cuba and Jamaica
† Visited in Jamaica by the Streamertail

PLUMBAGINACEAE   *Plumbago scandens*
Leadwort, Wild Plumbago; White Plumbago, Doctor Bush (Bahamas); Higuillo, Meladillo
     Silvestre (Puerto Rico); Malacara, Pega Pollo (Cuba)
West Indies, including the Bahamas, Cuba, Jamaica, Puerto Rico, and Martinique
† Visited in Jamaica by the Streamertail and the Vervain Hummingbird

POLYGALACEAE   *Securidaca brownei*
Jamaica
† Visited by the Vervain Hummingbird

S. diversifolia
Maravedí (Cuba)
West Indies, including Cuba and Martinique

POLYGONACEAE   *Coccoloba sintenisii*
Uvero de Monte
Puerto Rico—endemic
* Pollinated by the Puerto Rican Emerald

ROSACEAE   *Rubus rosifolius*
Frambuesa Común, Fresa, Rosa de Novia, Zaza, Mountain Raspberry, Wild Raspberry (Puerto
     Rico)
Puerto Rico
* Pollinated by the Puerto Rican Emerald
Rubus sp.
Bramble
Jamaica
† Visited by the Streamertail

RUBIACEAE   *Cephaelis elata*
Jamaica
† Visited by the Streamertail and the Vervain Hummingbird

Coffea arabica
Coffee; Café (Spanish)
Jamaica and Puerto Rico
* Pollinated in Puerto Rico by the Puerto Rican Emerald
† Visited in Jamaica by the Streamertail and the Jamaican Mango

Duggena hirsuta
Mata de Mariposa, Palo Pelado, Rabo de Ratón, Yerba Pelada (Puerto Rico)
Puerto Rico
* Pollinated by the Puerto Rican Emerald

Hamelia cuprea
Ponasí (Cuba)
Cuba, Jamaica, Haiti, Dominican Republic, and Grand Cayman
† Visited in Jamaica by the Streamertail

H. patens
Scarlet Bush, Scarlet Hamelia, Firebush; Scarlet Hamelia (Bahamas); Bálsamo, Scarletbush,
     Bálsamo Colorado, Pata de Pájaro (Puerto Rico); Buzunuvo, Desyerba Conuco, Buzunuco
     (Dominican Republic); Ponasí, Coralillo, Palo Coral (Cuba); Corail (Haiti)
The Bahamas; Greater Antilles, including Cuba, Haiti, Dominican Republic, and Puerto Rico;
     Lesser Antilles, including the Virgin Islands, St. Kitts, Guadeloupe, Dominica, Martinique,
     and St. Vincent

Female Bee Hummingbird/Flame of the Woods (Ixora coccinea). *Playa Larga, Ciénega de Zapata, Cuba.*

* Pollinated in Puerto Rico by the Puerto Rican Emerald, the Green Mango, and the Antillean Mango
† Visited in Cuba by the Bee Hummingbird
† Visited in the Dominican Republic by the Antillean Mango and the Vervain Hummingbird

Ixora coccinea
Flame of the Woods, Jungle Flame, Jungle Geranium; Cruz de Malta (Puerto Rico); Ixora (Cuba); Corail (Martinique)
Cuba, Jamaica, Puerto Rico, and Martinique
† Visited in Cuba by the Bee Hummingbird
† Visited in Jamaica by the Vervain Hummingbird
† Visited in Martinique by the Antillean Crested Hummingbird

I. macrothyrsa
King Ixora, Super King, Jungle Flame; Cruz de Malta (Puerto Rico)
Puerto Rico and Martinique
† Visited in Puerto Rico by the Antillean Crested Hummingbird
† Visited in Martinique by the Antillean Crested Hummingbird

Ixora sp.
Jamaica

Morinda royoc
Red Gal, Strongback; Rhubarb, Wild Mulberry (Bahamas); Pinipiní, Garanón (Cuba)
The Bahamas, Cuba, Jamaica, Haiti, Dominican Republic, and Grand Cayman
† Visited in Jamaica by the Vervain Hummingbird

Palicourea crocea
Cachimbo, Red Palicourea (Puerto Rico); Tapa Camino, Ponasí (Cuba); Bois de l'Encore, Bois Cabrit, Bois Fou-fou (Martinique)
West Indies, including Cuba, Jamaica, Haiti, Dominican Republic, Puerto Rico, and the Lesser Antilles from Guadeloupe southward
* Pollinated in Puerto Rico by the Puerto Rican Emerald

P. crocea var. *riparia*
Tapa Camino
Puerto Rico
† Visited by the Puerto Rican Emerald

Pentas lanceolata
Star-cluster, Egyptian Star-cluster; Pentas (Cuba); Maladrière, Fleur à Diable, Corbeille d'Argent (French)
Cuba

Pentas sp.
Jamaica

Psychotria corymbosa
Wild Coffee
Jamaica
† Visited by the Streamertail

P. pubescens
Hairy Wild Coffee (Bahamas); Cachimbo (Puerto Rico)
The Bahamas; Greater Antilles, including Jamaica and Puerto Rico; St. Thomas and St. Kitts
† Visited in Jamaica by the Streamertail

SCROPHULARIACEAE **Russelia equisetiformis**
Mare's Tail, Coral Plant, Fountain Plant, Fountain Bush, Figwort, Glass-eye Berry; Russellia
    (Bahamas); Lagrimas de Cupido (Cuba); Goutte de Sang, Queue de Cheval, Cloche de
    Corneville (Martinique)
West Indies, including the Bahamas, Cuba, Jamaica, Dominican Republic, Martinique, and
    Grand Cayman
† Visited in the Bahamas by the Bahama Woodstar
† Visited in Jamaica by the Streamertail and the Vervain Hummingbird
† Visited in Cuba by the Bee Hummingbird and the Cuban Emerald
† Visited in the Dominican Republic by the Antillean Mango and the Vervain Hummingbird

Immature male Vervain
Hummingbird/Coral Plant (Russelia
equisetiformis). *Kingston, Jamaica.*

SOLANACEAE   *Brugmansia suaveolens*
Angel's Trumpet; Campana (Cuba)
Cuba and Jamaica

Cestrum macrophyllum
Galan del Monte (Puerto Rico)
Puerto Rico
† Visited by the Puerto Rican Emerald

Dunalia arborescens
Gallinero, Alelí Falso, Trompeta de Ángel, Tulipán Sencillo (Puerto Rico); Dama de la Noche
    (Cuba); Aguacero, Dama de Noche (Dominican Republic); Fleur Trompette (Martinique);
    Galán, Lady-of-the-Night (Dutch Antilles); Rain-Tree, Empoisonneur (Dominica)
Cuba, Jamaica, Haiti, Dominican Republic, Puerto Rico, and the Virgin Islands southward to
    the Lesser Antilles
† Visited in Jamaica by the Streamertail and the Vervain Hummingbird

Nicotiana tabacum
Common Tobacco, Tobacco; Tabaco (Cuba)
The Bahamas, Cuba, and Puerto Rico
† Visited in Puerto Rico by the Green Mango

TROPAEOLACEAE   *Tropaeolum majus*
Garden Nasturtium, Tall Nasturtium, Indian Cress
Cuba and Jamaica

VERBENACEAE   *Citharexylum spinosum*
Fiddlewood; Péndula, Susanna (Puerto Rico); Susanna, Fiddlewood (Virgin Islands); Cotelette
    (Grenada); Bois Cotelette (Dominica, Martinique, St. Lucia); Bois Guitare, Bois de Fer
    Blanc (Guadeloupe); Susanna-berry (Dutch Antilles)
Puerto Rico, Cuba, St. Croix, St. Thomas, and the Lesser Antilles from Saba to Barbados

Clerodendrum paniculatum
Arbre Pagode
Martinique

C. thomsoniae
Rice and Peas, Bleeding Glory Bower, Tropical Bleeding Heart, Bleeding Heart Vine, Glory
    Tree, Bagflower; Coeur de Marie (French)
Jamaica

Duranta erecta
Cuba
† Visited by the Bee Hummingbird

Holmskioldia sanguinea
Chinese Hat, Chinese Hat Plant, Japanese Hat, Mandarin's Hat, Cup and Saucer Plant; Farolito
    Japonés (Cuba); Chapeau Chinois (Martinique)
Cuba, Jamaica, and Martinique
† Visited in Jamaica by the Vervain Hummingbird
† Visited in Martinique by the Antillean Crested Hummingbird

Lantana camara
Yellow Sage, Shrub Verbena, White Sage, Wild Sage; Cariaquillo (Puerto Rico); Filigrana
    (Cuba); Vieille Fille, Melle Marie Derrière l'Hôpital, Mille Fleurs (French)
Cuba, Jamaica, Puerto Rico, St. Lucia, Martinique, and Grenada
† Visited in Jamaica by the Streamertail and the Vervain Hummingbird
† Visited in Puerto Rico by the Puerto Rican Emerald and the Antillean Crested Hummingbird
† Visited in St. Lucia by the Antillean Crested Hummingbird
† Visited in Martinique by the Antillean Crested Hummingbird
† Visited in Grenada by the Antillean Crested Hummingbird

L. montevidensis
Weeping Lantana, Trailing Lantana, Polecat Geranium; Vieille Fille, Melle Marie Derrière
    l'Hôpital, Mille Fleurs (Martinique)
Martinique
† Visited by the Antillean Crested Hummingbird

Lantana sp.
Jamaica and Dominica
† Visited in Jamaica by the Streamertail
† Visited in Dominica by the Green-throated Carib and the Antillean Crested Hummingbird

Female Bee Hummingbird/Duranta erecta. *Santo Tomás, Ciénega de Zapata, Cuba.*

Immature male Vervain Hummingbird/Japanese Hat (Holmskioldia sanguinea). *Kingston, Jamaica.*

Lippia alba
Colic Mint, Cullen Mint, Guinea Mint; Salvia Americana, Quita Dolor (Cuba)
West Indies, including Cuba, Puerto Rico, Martinique, and Grand Cayman

Nyctanthes arbor-tristis
Night Jasmine, Tree of Sadness, Night-Blooming Jasmine
Jamaica
† Visited in Jamaica by the Vervain Hummingbird

Stachytarpheta cayennensis
Verbena Cimarrona (Cuba)
West Indies, including Cuba, Jamaica, and Martinique

S. jamaicensis
Porter Weed, Vervine; Jamaica Vervain, Blue Flower (Bahamas); Verbena (Puerto Rico);
    Verbena Azul (Cuba)
West Indies, including the Bahamas, Cuba, Jamaica, Puerto Rico, St. Lucia, and Grand Cayman
† Visited in the Bahamas by the Bahama Woodstar
† Visited in St. Lucia by the Antillean Crested Hummingbird

S. mutabilis
Cuba, Jamaica, Haiti, and the Dominican Republic
† Visited in Jamaica by the Streamertail

*H*ummingbird-Pollinated Flowers

MONOCOTYLEDONS

BROMELIACEAE   *Guzmania berteroniana*
* Pollinated in Puerto Rico by the Green Mango

Hohenbergia portorricensis
* Pollinated in Puerto Rico by the Puerto Rican Emerald

Pitcairnia bromeliifolia
* Pollinated in Puerto Rico by the Green Mango and the Antillean Mango

Tillandsia utriculata
* Pollinated in Puerto Rico by the Green Mango and the Antillean Mango

Vriesea sintenisii
* Pollinated in Puerto Rico by the Puerto Rican Emerald

MUSACEAE   *Musa* x *paradisiaca*
* Pollinated in Puerto Rico by the Puerto Rican Emerald, the Green Mango, and the Antillean
  Mango

ORCHIDACEAE   *Dilomilis montana*
* Pollinated in Puerto Rico by the Puerto Rican Emerald

Epidendrum sp.
* Pollinated in Puerto Rico by the Puerto Rican Emerald

ZINGIBERACEAE   *Hedychium coronarium*
* Pollinated in Puerto Rico by the Puerto Rican Emerald

Renealmia antillarum
* Pollinated in Puerto Rico by the Puerto Rican Emerald, the Green Mango, and the Antillean
  Mango

DICOTYLEDONS

ACANTHACEAE   *Justicia martinsoniana*
* Pollinated in Puerto Rico by the Puerto Rican Emerald

Ruellia coccinea
* Pollinated in Puerto Rico by the Puerto Rican Emerald

Sanchezia nobilis
* Pollinated in Puerto Rico by the Puerto Rican Emerald

Thunbergia erecta
* Pollinated in Puerto Rico by the Green Mango

ANACARDIACEAE *Anacardium occidentale*
* Pollinated in Puerto Rico by the Puerto Rican Emerald

ASCLEPIADACEAE *Asclepias curassavica*
* Pollinated in Puerto Rico by the Puerto Rican Emerald

BALSAMINACEAE *Impatiens suttonii*
* Pollinated in Puerto Rico by the Puerto Rican Emerald

BIGNONIACEAE *Spathodea campanulata*
* Pollinated in Puerto Rico by the Puerto Rican Emerald and the Green Mango

Tabebuia haemantha
* Pollinated in Puerto Rico by the Puerto Rican Emerald, the Green Mango, and the Antillean
Mango

T. rigida
* Pollinated in Puerto Rico by the Green Mango

T. schumanniana
* Pollinated in Puerto Rico by the Puerto Rican Emerald, the Green Mango, and the Antillean
Mango

BORAGINACEAE *Cordia collococca*
* Pollinated in Puerto Rico by the Puerto Rican Emerald

C. rickseckeri
* Pollinated in Puerto Rico by the Green Mango and the Antillean Mango

CACTACEAE *Melocactus intortus*
* Pollinated in Puerto Rico by the Puerto Rican Emerald and the Antillean Mango

CAESALPINIACEAE *Bauhinia monandra*
* Pollinated in Puerto Rico by the Puerto Rican Emerald and the Green Mango

Delonix regia
* Pollinated in Puerto Rico by the Puerto Rican Emerald

CHRYSOBALANACEAE *Hirtella rugosa*
* Pollinated in Puerto Rico by the Puerto Rican Emerald

COMPOSITAE *Clibadium erosum*
(ASTERACEAE) * Pollinated in Puerto Rico by the Puerto Rican Emerald

Piptocarpha tetrantha
* Pollinated in Puerto Rico by the Puerto Rican Emerald

CONVOLVULACEAE *Ipomoea arenaria*
* Pollinated in Puerto Rico by the Green Mango and the Antillean Mango

I. repanda
* Pollinated in Puerto Rico by the Puerto Rican Emerald, Green Mango, and the Antillean
Mango

EUPHORBIACEAE *Acalypha wilkesiana*
* Pollinated in Puerto Rico by the Puerto Rican Emerald

GENTIANACEAE   *Lisianthius laxiflorus*
                  * Pollinated in Puerto Rico by the Puerto Rican Emerald

GESNERIACEAE   *Gesneria pedunculosa*
                  * Pollinated in Puerto Rico by the Puerto Rican Emerald

GUTTIFERAE   *Clusia krugiana*
                  * Pollinated in Puerto Rico by the Puerto Rican Emerald

                  C. minor
                  * Pollinated in Puerto Rico by the Puerto Rican Emerald

LABIATAE   *Plectranthus blumei*
(LAMIACEAE)   * Pollinated in Puerto Rico by the Puerto Rican Emerald

LOBELIACEAE   *Lobelia portorricensis*
                  * Pollinated in Puerto Rico by the Puerto Rican Emerald

LYTHRACEAE   *Lagerstroemia speciosa*
                  * Pollinated in Puerto Rico by the Puerto Rican Emerald

MALVACEAE   *Hibiscus rosa-sinensis*
                  * Pollinated in Puerto Rico by the Puerto Rican Emerald and the Green Mango

MARCGRAVIACEAE   *Marcgravia rectiflora*
                  * Pollinated in Puerto Rico by the Puerto Rican Emerald

                  M. sintenisii
                  * Pollinated in Puerto Rico by the Puerto Rican Emerald

MELASTOMATACEAE   *Heterotrichum cymosum*
                  * Pollinated in Puerto Rico by the Puerto Rican Emerald

                  Mecranium amygdalinum
                  * Pollinated in Puerto Rico by the Puerto Rican Emerald

                  Miconia sp.
                  * Pollinated in Puerto Rico by the Puerto Rican Emerald

MIMOSACEAE   *Inga vera*
                  * Pollinated in Puerto Rico by the Puerto Rican Emerald

MYRTACEAE   *Syzygium jambos*
                  * Pollinated in Puerto Rico by the Puerto Rican Emerald and the Green Mango
                  S. malaccense
                  * Pollinated in Puerto Rico by the Puerto Rican Emerald and the Green Mango

PAPILIONACEAE   *Erythrina berteroana*
(FABACEAE)   * Pollinated in Puerto Rico by the Green Mango

                  Neorudolphia volubilis
                  * Pollinated in Puerto Rico by the Green Mango and the Antillean Mango

                  Sabinea punicea
                  * Pollinated in Puerto Rico by the Puerto Rican Emerald, the Green Mango, and the Antillean
                      Mango

POLYGONACEAE   *Coccoloba sintenisii*
                  * Pollinated in Puerto Rico by the Puerto Rican Emerald

ROSACEAE   *Rubus rosifolius*
* Pollinated in Puerto Rico by the Puerto Rican Emerald

RUBIACEAE   *Coffea arabica*
* Pollinated in Puerto Rico by the Puerto Rican Emerald

Duggena hirsuta
* Pollinated in Puerto Rico by the Puerto Rican Emerald

Hamelia patens
* Pollinated in Puerto Rico by the Puerto Rican Emerald, the Green Mango, and the Antillean Mango

Palicourea crocea
* Pollinated in Puerto Rico by the Puerto Rican Emerald

Hummingbirds of the World 6

Twenty-nine hummingbirds are on the endangered species list and, because of the rapid destruction of their habitat, may one day be extinct. An asterisk (*) denotes these endangered species.

Doryfera
   johannae — Blue-fronted Lancebill
   ludovicae — Green-fronted Lancebill
Androdon
   aequatorialis — Tooth-billed Hummingbird
Ramphodon
   naevius — Saw-billed Hermit
Glaucis
   *dohrnii — Hook-billed Hermit
   aenea — Bronzy Hermit
   hirsuta — Rufous-breasted Hermit
Threnetes
   niger — Sooty Barbthroat
   loehkeni — Bronze-tailed Barbthroat
   leucurus — Pale-tailed Barbthroat
   ruckeri — Band-tailed Barbthroat
Phaethornis
   yaruqui — White-whiskered Hermit
   guy — Green Hermit
   syrmatophorus — Tawny-bellied Hermit
   superciliosus — Long-tailed Hermit
   malaris — Great-billed Hermit
   margarettae — Margaretta Hermit
   eurynome — Scale-throated Hermit
   *nigrirostris — Black-billed Hermit
   hispidus — White-bearded Hermit
   anthophilus — Pale-bellied Hermit
   bourcieri — Straight-billed Hermit
   philippii — Needle-billed Hermit
   squalidus — Dusky-throated Hermit
   augusti — Sooty-capped Hermit
   pretrei — Planalto Hermit
   subochraceus — Buff-bellied Hermit
   nattereri — Cinnamon-throated Hermit
   maranhaoensis — Maranhão Hermit
   gounellei — Broad-tipped Hermit
   ruber — Reddish Hermit
   stuarti — White-browed Hermit
   griseogularis — Gray-chinned Hermit
   longuemareus — Little Hermit
   idaliae — Minute Hermit
Eutoxeres
   aquila — White-tipped Sicklebill
   condamini — Buff-tailed Sicklebill
Phaeochroa
   cuvierii — Scaly-breasted Hummingbird
Campylopterus
   curvipennis — Wedge-tailed Sabrewing
   largipennis — Gray-breasted Sabrewing
   rufus — Rufous Sabrewing
   hyperythrus — Rufous-breasted Sabrewing
   duidae — Buff-breasted Sabrewing
   hemileucurus — Violet Sabrewing
   *ensipennis — White-tailed Sabrewing
   falcatus — Lazuline Sabrewing
   phainopeplus — Santa Marta Sabrewing
   villaviscensio — Napo Sabrewing
Eupetomena
   macroura — Swallow-tailed Hummingbird
Florisuga
   mellivora — White-necked Jacobin
Melanotrochilus
   fuscus — Black Jacobin
Colibri
   delphinae — Brown Violet-ear
   thalassinus — Green Violet-ear
   coruscans — Sparkling Violet-ear
   serrirostris — White-vented Violet-ear

Anthracothorax		
viridigula	Green-throated Mango	
prevostii	Green-breasted Mango	
nigricollis	Black-throated Mango	
veraguensis	Veraguan Mango	
dominicus	Antillean Mango	
viridis	Green Mango	
mango	Jamaican Mango	
Avocettula		
recurvirostris	Fiery-tailed Awlbill	
Eulampis		
holosericeus	Green-throated Carib	
jugularis	Purple-throated Carib	
Chrysolampis		
mosquitus	Ruby-topaz Hummingbird	
Orthorhyncus		
cristatus	Antillean Crested Hummingbird	
Klais		
guimeti	Violet-headed Hummingbird	
Abeillia		
abeillei	Emerald-chinned Hummingbird	
Stephanoxis		
lalandi	Black-breasted Plovercrest	
Lophornis		
ornata	Tufted Coquette	
gouldii	Dot-eared Coquette	
magnifica	Frilled Coquette	
delattrei	Rufous-crested Coquette	
stictolopha	Spangled Coquette	
melaniae	Dusky Coquette	
chalybea	Festive Coquette	
pavonina	Peacock Coquette	
insignibarbis	Bearded Coquette	
Paphosia		
helenae	Black-crested Coquette	
adorabilis	White-crested Coquette	
Popelairia		
popelairii	Wire-crested Thorntail	
langsdorffi	Black-bellied Thorntail	
*letitiae	Coppery Thorntail	
conversii	Green Thorntail	
Discosura		
longicauda	Racket-tailed Coquette	
Chlorestes		
notatus	Blue-chinned Sapphire	
Chlorostilbon		
mellisugus	Blue-tailed Emerald	
aureoventris	Glittering Emerald	
canivetii	Fork-tailed Emerald	
ricordii	Cuban Emerald	

swainsonii	Hispaniolan Emerald	
maugaeus	Puerto Rican Emerald	
gibsoni	Red-billed Emerald	
russatus	Coppery Emerald	
inexpectatus	Berlepsch Emerald	
stenura	Narrow-tailed Emerald	
alice	Green-tailed Emerald	
poortmani	Short-tailed Emerald	
auratus	Cabanis Emerald	
Cynanthus		
sordidus	Dusky Hummingbird	
latirostris	Broad-billed Hummingbird	
Ptochoptera		
iolaima	Natterer Emerald	
Cyanophaia		
bicolor	Blue-headed Hummingbird	
Thalurania		
furcata	Crowned (Fork-tailed) Woodnymph	
watertonii	Long-tailed Woodnymph	
glaucopis	Violet-capped Woodnymph	
lerchi	Lerch Woodnymph	
Augasmall		
cyaneoberyllina	Berlioz Woodnymph	
smaragdinea	Emerald Woodnymph	
Neoleshia		
nehrkorni	Nehrkorn Hummingbird	
Panterpe		
insignis	Fiery-throated Hummingbird	
Damophila		
julie	Violet-bellied Hummingbird	
Lepidopyga		
coeruleogularis	Sapphire-throated Hummingbird	
*lilliae	Sapphire-bellied Hummingbird	
goudoti	Shining-green Hummingbird	
Hylocharis		
(Basilinna)		
xantusii	Black-fronted Hummingbird	
leucotis	White-eared Hummingbird	
(Hylocharis)		
eliciae	Blue-throated Goldentail	
sapphirina	Rufous-throated Sapphire	
cyanus	White-chinned Sapphire	
pyropygia	Flame-rumped Sapphire	
chrysura	Gilded Hummingbird	
(Eucephala)		
grayi	Blue-headed Sapphire	
Chrysuronia		
oenone	Golden-tailed Sapphire	
Goldmania		
violiceps	Violet-capped Hummingbird	

Goethalsia	
bella	Pirre Hummingbird
Trochilus	
polytmus	Western Streamertail
scitulus	Eastern Streamertail
Leucochloris	
albicollis	White-throated Hummingbird
Polytmus	
guainumbi	White-tailed Goldenthroat
milleri	Tepui Goldenthroat
theresiae	Green-tailed Goldenthroat
Leucippus	
fallax	Buffy Hummingbird
baeri	Tumbes Hummingbird
taczanowskii	Spot-throated Hummingbird
chlorocercus	Olive-spotted Hummingbird
Taphrospilus	
hypostictus	Many-spotted Hummingbird
Amazilia	
(Chionogaster)	
chionogaster	White-bellied Hummingbird
viridicauda	Green-and-white Hummingbird
(Polyerata)	
candida	White-bellied Emerald
chionopectus	White-chested Emerald
versicolor	Versicolored Emerald
*luciae	Honduras Emerald
fimbriata	Glittering-throated Emerald
*distans	Tachira Emerald
lactea	Sapphire-spangled Emerald
amabilis	Blue-chested Hummingbird
cyaneotincta	Blue-spotted Hummingbird
rosenbergi	Purple-chested Hummingbird
*boucardi	Mangrove Hummingbird
franciae	Andean Emerald
leucogaster	Plain-bellied Emerald
cyanocephala	Red-billed Azurecrown
microrhyncha	Small-billed Azurecrown
(Saucerottia)	
cyanifrons	Indigo-capped Hummingbird
beryllina	Berylline Hummingbird
cyanura	Blue-tailed Hummingbird
saucerrottei	Steely-vented Hummingbird
tobaci	Copper-rumped Hummingbird
viridigaster	Green-bellied Hummingbird
edward	Snowy-breasted Hummingbird
(Amazilia)	
rutila	Cinnamon Hummingbird
yucatanensis	Buff-bellied Hummingbird
tzacatl	Rufous-tailed Hummingbird
handleyi	Escudo Hummingbird

*castaneiventris	Chestnut-bellied Hummingbird
amazilia	Amazilia Hummingbird
viridifrons	Green-fronted Hummingbird
violiceps	Violet-crowned Hummingbird
Eupherusa	
*poliocerca	White-tailed Hummingbird
eximia	Stripe-tailed Hummingbird
*cyanophrys	Blue-capped (Oaxaca) Hummingbird
nigriventris	Black-bellied Hummingbird
Elvira	
chionura	White-tailed Emerald
cupreiceps	Coppery-headed Emerald
Microchera	
albocoronata	Snowcap
Chalybura	
buffonii	White-vented Plumeleteer
urochrysia	Bronze-tailed Plumeleteer
Aphantochroa	
cirrochloris	Sombre Hummingbird
Lampornis	
clemenciae	Blue-throated Hummingbird
amethystinus	Amethyst-throated Hummingbird
viridipallens	Green-throated Mountain-gem
hemileucus	White-bellied Mountain-gem
castaneoventris	White-throated (Variable) Mountain-gem
cinereicauda	Gray-tailed Mountain-gem
Lamprolaima	
rhami	Garnet-throated Hummingbird
Adelomyia	
melanogenys	Speckled Hummingbird
Anthocephala	
floriceps	Blossomcrown
Urosticte	
benjamini	Whitetip
Phlogophilus	
hemileucurus	Ecuadorean Piedtail
harterti	Peruvian Piedtail
Clytolaema	
rubricauda	Brazilian Ruby
Polyplancta	
aurescens	Gould Jewelfront
Heliodoxa	
rubinoides	Fawn-breasted Brilliant
leadbeateri	Violet-fronted Brilliant
jacula	Green-crowned Brilliant
xanthogonys	Velvet-browed Brilliant
schreibersii	Black-throated Brilliant
gularis	Pink-throated Brilliant

branickii	Rufous-webbed Brilliant	
imperatrix	Empress Brilliant	
Eugenes		
fulgens	Magnificent (Rivoli) Hummingbird	
Hylonympha		
macrocerca	Scissor-tailed Hummingbird	
Sternoclyta		
cyanopectus	Violet-chested Hummingbird	
Topaza		
pella	Crimson Topaz	
pyra	Fiery Topaz	
Oreotrochilus		
melanogaster	Black-breasted Hillstar	
estella	Andean Hillstar	
leucopleurus	White-sided Hillstar	
adela	Wedge-tailed Hillstar	
Urochroa		
bougueri	White-tailed Hillstar	
Patagona		
gigas	Giant Hummingbird	
Aglaeactis		
cupripennis	Shining Sunbeam	
aliciae	Purple-backed Sunbeam	
castelnaudii	White-tufted Sunbeam	
pamela	Black-hooded Sunbeam	
Lafresnaya		
lafresnayi	Mountain Velvetbreast	
Pterophanes		
cyanopterus	Great Sapphirewing	
Coeligena		
coeligena	Bronzy Inca	
wilsoni	Brown Inca	
prunellei	Black Inca	
torquata	Collared Inca	
phalerata	White-tailed Starfrontlet	
bonapartei	Golden-bellied Starfrontlet	
orina	Dusky Starfrontlet	
helianthea	Blue-throated Starfrontlet	
lutetiae	Buff-winged Starfrontlet	
violifer	Violet-throated Starfrontlet	
iris	Rainbow Starfrontlet	
Ensifera		
ensifera	Sword-billed Hummingbird	
Sephanoides		
sephanoides	Green-backed Firecrown	
fernandensis	Juan Fernandez Firecrown	
Boissonneaua		
flavescens	Buff-tailed Coronet	
matthewsii	Chestnut-breasted Coronet	
jardini	Velvet-purple Coronet	
Heliangelus		
mavors	Orange-throated Sunangel	
spencei	Merida Sunangel	

amethysticollis	Amethyst-throated Sunangel	
strophianus	Gorgeted Sunangel	
exortis	Tourmaline Sunangel	
viola	Purple-throated Sunangel	
micraster	Little Sunangel	
squamigularis	Olive-throated Sunangel	
speciosa	Green-throated Sunangel	
rothschildi	Rothschild Sunangel	
luminosus	Glistening Sunangel	
Eriocnemis		
nigrivestis	Black-breasted Puffleg	
soderstromi	Söderström Puffleg	
vestitus	Glowing Puffleg	
godini	Turquoise-throated Puffleg	
cupreoventris	Coppery-bellied Puffleg	
luciani	Sapphire-vented Puffleg	
isaacsonii	Isaacson Puffleg	
mosquera	Golden-breasted Puffleg	
glaucopoides	Blue-capped Puffleg	
mirabilis	Colorful Puffleg	
alinae	Emerald-bellied Puffleg	
derbyi	Black-thighed Puffleg	
Haplophaedia		
aureliae	Greenish Puffleg	
lugens	Hoary Puffleg	
Ocreatus		
underwoodii	Booted Racket-tail	
Lesbia		
victoriae	Black-tailed Trainbearer	
nuna	Green-tailed Trainbearer	
Sappho		
sparganura	Red-tailed Comet	
Polyonymus		
caroli	Bronze-tailed Comet	
Zodalia		
glyceria	Purple-tailed Comet	
Ramphomicron		
microrhynchum	Purple-backed Thornbill	
dorsale	Black-backed Thornbill	
Metallura		
phoebe	Black Metaltail	
theresiae	Coppery Metaltail	
purpureicauda	Purple-tailed Thornbill	
aeneocauda	Scaled Metaltail	
baroni	Violet-throated Metaltail	
eupogon	Fire-throated Metaltail	
williami	Viridian Metaltail	
tyrianthina	Tyrian Metaltail	
iracunda	Perija Metaltail	
Chalcostigma		
ruficeps	Rufous-capped Thornbill	
olivaceum	Olivaceous Thornbill	
stanleyi	Blue-mantled Thornbill	
heteropogon	Bronze-tailed Thornbill	

herrani	Rainbow-bearded Thornbill	*pulcher*	Beautiful Hummingbird
Oxypogon		Archilochus	
guerinii	Bearded Helmetcrest	*colubris*	Ruby-throated Hummingbird
Opisthoprora		*alexandri*	Black-chinned Hummingbird
euryptera	Mountain Avocetbill	Calliphlox	
Taphrolesbia		*evelynae*	Bahama Woodstar
griseiventris	Gray-bellied Comet	*bryantae*	Magenta-throated Woodstar
Aglaiocercus		*amethystina*	Amethyst Woodstar
kingi	Long-tailed Sylph	Mellisuga	
coelestis	Violet-tailed Sylph	*minima*	Vervain Hummingbird
Oreonympha		*helenae*	Bee Hummingbird
nobilis	Bearded Mountaineer	Calypte	
Augastes		*anna*	Anna's Hummingbird
scutatus	Hyacinth Visorbearer	*costae*	Costa's Hummingbird
lumachellus	Hooded Visorbearer	Stellula	
Schistes		*calliope*	Calliope Hummingbird
geoffroyi	Wedge-billed Hummingbird	Atthis	
Heliothryx		*heloisa*	Bumblebee Hummingbird
barroti	Purple-crowned Fairy	*ellioti*	Wine-throated Hummingbird
aurita	Black-eared Fairy	Myrtis	
Heliactin		*fanny*	Purple-collared Woodstar
cornuta	Horned Sungem	Eulidia	
Loddigesia		*yarrellii*	Chilean Woodstar
mirabilis	Marvellous Spatuletail	Myrmia	
Heliomaster		*micrura*	Short-tailed Woodstar
constantii	Plain-capped Starthroat	Acestrura	
longirostris	Long-billed Starthroat	*mulsant*	White-bellied Woodstar
squamosus	Stripe-breasted Starthroat	*decorata*	Decorated Woodstar
furcifer	Blue-tufted Starthroat	*bombus*	Little Woodstar
Rhodopis		*heliodor*	Gorgeted Woodstar
vesper	Oasis Hummingbird	*berlepschi*	Esmeralda Woodstar
Thaumastura		*harterti*	Hartert Woodstar
cora	Peruvian Sheartail	Chaetocercus	
Philodice		*jourdanii*	Rufous-shafted Woodstar
mitchellii	Purple-throated Woodstar	Selasphorus	
Doricha		*platycercus*	Broad-tailed Hummingbird
enicura	Slender Sheartail	*rufus*	Rufous Hummingbird
eliza	Mexican Sheartail	*sasin*	Allen's Hummingbird
Tilmatura		*flammula*	Volcano (Rose-throated) Hummingbird
dupontii	Sparkling-tailed (Dupont) Hummingbird	*torridus*	Heliotrope-throated Hummingbird
Microstilbon		*simoni*	Cerise-throated Hummingbird
burmeisteri	Slender-tailed Woodstar	*ardens*	Glow-throated Hummingbird
Calothorax		*scintilla*	Scintillant Hummingbird
lucifer	Lucifer Hummingbird		

*B*ibliography

A., H. D. 1914. (Notes) Humming birds. *Avicultural Magazine* 5:88.

Adams, C. D. 1972. *Flowering plants of Jamaica.* University of the West Indies, Mona, Jamaica.

Allen, J. A. 1900. Supplementary notes on birds collected in the Santa Marta District, Colombia, by Herbert H. Smith, with descriptions of nests and eggs. *Bulletin of the American Museum of Natural History* 21:281.

American Ornithologists' Union (AOU). 1983. *Check-list of North American birds.* 6th ed. American Ornithologists' Union [Washington, D.C.].

Arendt, W., and J. Faaborg. Letter to author, 15 May 1988.

Astley, H. D. 1914. Powers of resuscitation in humming birds. *Avicultural Magazine* 5:339–40.

Atlas of the United States and The World. George Philip Ltd., 1987.

Barbour, T. 1923. The birds of Cuba. *Memoirs of the Nuttall Ornithological Club* 6:1–130.

———. 1943. Cuban ornithology. *Memoirs of the Nuttall Ornithological Club* 9:1–129.

———. 1946. *A naturalist in Cuba.* Little, Brown & Co., Boston.

Belcher, C., and G. D. Smooker. 1936. Birds of the colony of Trinidad and Tobago. *Ibis* 6:28–29.

Biaggi, V. 1970. *Las aves de Puerto Rico.* Editorial Universitaria/Universidad de Puerto Rico, Rio Piedras.

Bisse, J. 1981. *Arboles de Cuba.* Editorial Cientifico-Tecnica, Havana.

Blake, C. H. 1956. Observations on the Streamer-tailed hummingbird. *Bird-banding* 27:181.

Bond, J. 1928a. The distribution and habits of the birds of the Republic of Haiti. *Proceedings of the Academy of Natural Sciences of Philadelphia* 80:483–521.

———. 1928b. On the birds of Dominica, St. Lucia, St. Vincent, and Barbadoes, B.W.I. *Proceedings of the Academy of Natural Sciences of Philadelphia* 80:523–45.

———. 1936. *Birds of the West Indies.* Academy of Natural Sciences of Philadelphia.

———. 1941. Nidification of the birds of Dominica, B.W.I. *Auk* 58:364–75.

———. 1942. Additional notes on West Indian Birds. *Proceedings of the Academy of Natural Sciences of Philadelphia* 94:89–106.

———. 1945. *Check-list of birds of the West Indies.* 2d ed. Academy of Natural Sciences of Philadelphia.

———. 1948. Origin of the bird fauna of the W.I. *Wilson Bulletin* 60(4): 207–29.

———. 1950. Results of the Catherwood–Chaplin West Indies Expedition, 1948. Part 2, Birds of Cayo Largo (Cuba), San Andres and Providencia. *Proceedings of the Academy of Natural Sciences of Philadelphia* 102:43–68.

———. 1956. *Check-list of birds of the West Indies.* 4th ed. Academy of Natural Sciences of Philadelphia.

———. 1956. *First supplement to the check-list of birds of the West Indies.* Academy of Natural Sciences of Philadelphia.

———. 1956. *Third supplement to the check-list of birds of the West Indies.* Academy of Natural Sciences of Philadelphia.

———. 1956. *Fourth supplement to the check-list of birds of the West Indies.* Academy of Natural Sciences of Philadelphia.

———. 1956. *Tenth supplement to the check-list of birds of the West Indies.* Academy of Natural Sciences of Philadelphia.

———. 1956. *Eleventh supplement to the check-list of birds of the West Indies.* Academy of Natural Sciences of Philadelphia.

————. 1956. *Fifteenth supplement to the check-list of birds of the West Indies.* Academy of Natural Sciences of Philadelphia.

————. 1956. *Sixteenth supplement to the check-list of birds of the West Indies.* Academy of Natural Sciences of Philadelphia.

————. 1956. *Twentieth supplement to the check-list of birds of the West Indies.* Academy of Natural Sciences of Philadelphia.

————. 1956. *Twenty-third supplement to the check-list of birds of the West Indies.* Academy of Natural Sciences of Philadelphia.

————. 1956. *Twenty-seventh supplement to the check-list of birds of the West Indies.* Academy of Natural Sciences of Philadelphia.

————. 1963. Derivation of the Antillean avifauna. *Proceedings of the Academy of Natural Sciences of Philadelphia* 115:79–98.

————. 1966. Affinities of the Antillean avifauna. *Caribbean Journal of Science* 6 (3–4): 173–76.

————. 1969. Comments by distinguished visitors. *Gosse Bird Club Broadsheet* 13:12–13.

————. 1979. Derivations of Lesser Antillean birds. *Proceedings of the Academy of Natural Sciences of Philadelphia* 131:89–103.

————. 1985. *Birds of the West Indies.* 5th ed. Houghton Mifflin Company, Boston.

Bon Saint-Côme, M. 1982. Description du nid de *Cyanophaia bicolor* (Trochilide). *Oiseau* 52(4): 370–72.

Brewster, W., and O. Bangs. 1901. On an overlooked species of *Aithurus. Proceedings of the New England Zoological Club* 2:47–50.

Britton, N. L., and C. F. Millspaugh. 1920. *The Bahama flora.* New Era Printing Company, Lancaster, PA.

Brown, R. W. 1956. *Composition of scientific words.* Smithsonian Institution Press, Washington, D.C.

Brudenell-Bruce, P. G. C. 1975. *The Birds of New Providence and the Bahama Islands.* Collins, London.

Butler, A. L. 1926. Vitality of humming-bird chicks. *Ibis* 2:238.

Campbell, B., and E. Lack, eds. 1985. *A dictionary of birds.* Buteo Books, Vermillion, SD.

Carlquist, S. 1965. *Island life: A natural history of the islands of the world.* Natural History Press, Garden City, NY.

Chapman, F. M. 1891. The origin of the avifauna of the Bahamas. *American Naturalist* 25:528.

————. 1894. The birds of the island of Trinidad. *Bulletin of the American Museum of Natural History* 6:1–86.

Christy, C. 1897. Field-notes on the birds of the island of San Domingo. *Ibis* 3:317–330.

Columbus, Christopher. 1987. *The log of Christopher Columbus.* Translated by R. H. Fuson. International Marine Publishing Co., Camden, ME.

Conway, W. G. 1961. Hummingbirds with wrinkles. *Animal Kingdom* 65(4): 151–54.

Cory, C. B. 1885. *The birds of Haiti and San Domingo.* Estes & Lauriat, Boston.

————. 1890. *The birds of the Bahama Islands.* Estes & Lauriat, Boston.

Danforth, S. 1928. Birds observed in Jamaica in 1926. *Auk* 45:486.

————. 1929. Notes on the birds of Hispaniola. *Auk* 46:368–69.

————. 1934. The Birds of Antigua. *Auk* 51:35–364.

De La Sagra, D. R. 1855. Historia física, política y natural de la isla de Cuba. Vol. 2, *Primera parte—mamíferos y aves.* Imprenta de Maulde y Renou, Paris.

De Quincey, R. 1960. Notes on some humming birds—and the nesting of the Doctor, or Streamer-tailed Humming Bird. *Avicultural Magazine* 66:58–66.

Diamond, A. W. 1973. Habitats and feeding stations of St. Lucia forest birds. *Ibis* 155(3):313.

Dod, A. 1978. *Aves de la Republica Dominicana.* Editora Corripio, Santo Domingo.

Downer, A. 1972. Albino Streamertail. *Gosse Bird Club Broadsheet* 19:23.

————. 1973. Red-breasted hummingbirds. *Gosse Bird Club Broadsheet* 20:9–11.

Dusbabek, F., and V. Cerny. 1970. The nasal mites of Cuban birds. *Acarología* 12:269–81.

Emlen, J. T. 1973. Territorial aggression in wintering warblers at Bahama Agave blossoms. *Wilson Bulletin* 85(1): 71–74.

————. 1977. Land bird communities of Grand Bahama Island: The structure and dynamics of avifauna. *American Ornithologists' Union Monographs* 24:95.

————. 1981. Divergence in the foraging responses of birds on two Bahama islands. *Ecology* 62(2):189–295.

Ezra, A. 1943. Long-lived humming birds. *Avicultural Magazine* 5(8): 6–7.

Fernandez, E. 1972. *Art and mythology of the Taino Indians of the Greater West Indies.* Editorial Libros de Mexico, Mexico, D.F.

Fewkes, J. W. 1907. *The aborigines of Puerto Rico and neighboring islands.* 25th Annual Report, Bureau of American Ethnology, Smithsonian Institution, Washington, D.C.

ffrench, R. 1976. *A guide to the birds of Trinidad and Tobago.* Harrowood Books, Valley Forge, PA.

Fisk, E. 1974. Second U.S. record of a Bahama Woodstar. *American Bird* 28:855.

Garcia, A. 1965. *History of the West Indies.* George G. Harrap & Co., London.

Garcia, F. 1980. *Las aves de Cuba.* Tomo I, *Especies endémicas.* Editorial Gente Nueva, Havana.

Garrido, O. H., and F. Garcia Montana. 1975. *Catálogo de las aves de Cuba.* Academia de Ciencias de Cuba, Havana.

General Notes. 1956. *Gosse Bird Club Broadsheet* 5:17.

Gill, F. B., F. J. Stokes, and C. Stokes. 1973. Contact zones and hybridization in the Jamaican hummingbird, *Trochilus polytmus (L.). Condor* 75:170–76.

Gosse, P. H. 1847. *The birds of Jamaica.* John Van Voorst, Paternoster Row, London.

Graf, A. B. 1981. *Tropica, color cyclopedia of exotic plants and trees.* 2d ed. Roehrs Co., East Rutherford, NJ.

Griswold, O. 1960. Vervain Hummingbird: Second smallest bird in the world. *Animal Kingdom* 63:151–53.

Grzimek, B., ed. 1984. *Grzimek's Animal Life Encyclopedia.* Vol. 8, *Birds 2.* Van Nostrand Reinhold Company, New York.

Gundlach, J. 1898. *Ornitología Cubana o catálogo descriptivo de todas las especies de aves tanto indígenas como de paso anual o accidental observadas en 58 años.* Imprenta "La Moderna," Havana.

Hamel, P. B. Telephone conversation with authors, 21 September 1988.

Haverschmidt, F. 1968a. A nest of the Rufous-breasted Hermit with three eggs. *Auk* 85:693.

———. 1968b. *Birds of Surinam.* Oliver & Boyd, London.

Herklots, G. A. C. 1961. *Birds of Trinidad and Tobago.* Collins, London.

Hernandez-Prieto, E. 1985a. Patrón alimenticio de tres especies de aves nectarivoras en el roble de sierra *(Tabebuia rigida Urban: Bignoniaceae).* Paper presented at 6th Symposium of the Fauna of Puerto Rico and the Caribbean, 12 April, at Humacao University, Humacao, Puerto Rico.

———. 1985b. Feeding Activity of Nectarivores in a Puerto Rican Elfin Forest. Paper presented at 103rd Stated Meeting of the American Ornithologists' Union, 7–10 October, at Arizona State University, Tempe, Arizona.

———. 1986. Clave para la identificación de campo de los colibries presentes en Puerto Rico y algunas notas sobre estos. *Ornitologia Caribena* 2:27–34.

Heselton, H. C. 1903–04. Birds of Cuba and Jamaica. *Avicultural Magazine* 2:254–56.

Holmgren, V. C. 1986. *The way of the hummingbird.* Capra Press, Santa Barbara, California.

Howard, R. A. 1979. *Flora of the Lesser Antilles: Leeward and Windward Islands.* Vol. 3. Arnold Arboretum/Harvard University, Jamaica Plain, MA.

Ilichev, V. D., and A. V. Mikheev., eds. 1986. *Zhizń zhivotnyx* [The Lives of Animals]. Vol. 6, *Ptitsy* [Birds]. Prosveshchenie [Enlightenment], Moscow.

Ingels, J. 1976. Observations on some hummingbirds of Martinique. *Avicultural Magazine* 82:98–100.

Jeffrey-Smith, M. 1949. Bird notes. *Natural History Notes of the Natural History Society of Jamaica* 37:6.

———. 1956. *Bird-watching in Jamaica.* Pioneer Press, Kingston.

———. 1966. Vervain Hummingbird. *Gosse Bird Club Broadsheet* 7:19.

Johnsgard, P. 1983. *Hummingbirds of North America.* Smithsonian Institution Press, Washington, D.C.

Judge, J. 1986. Where Columbus found the New World. *National Geographic* 170(5): 566–99.

King, W. B., and A. T. Fenn. 1967. A short Jamaican bird-watching tour. *Gosse Bird Club Broadsheet* 9:9.

Kodric-Brown, A., J. H. Brown, G. S. Byers, and D. F. Gori. 1984. Organization of a tropical island community of hummingbirds and flowers. *Ecology* 65(5): 1358–68.

Lack, D. 1976. *Island biology: Illustrated by the land birds of Jamaica.* University of California Press, Berkeley.

Lack, D., and A. Lack. 1973. Birds on Grenada. *Ibis* 115(1): 53–59.

Lack, D., E. Lack, P. Lack, and A. Lack. 1973. Birds on St. Vincent. *Ibis* 115(1): 46–52.

Lambeye, J. 1850. *Aves de la isla de Cuba.* Imprenta del Tiempo, Havana.

Leck, C. F. 1973. Dominance relationships in nectar-feeding birds at St. Croix. *Auk* 90(2): 431–32.

Le Corre, G. 1985. *Fleurs des Tropiques.* Editions Exbrayat, Fort de France, Martinique.

Levi-Strauss, C. 1969. *The raw and the cooked.* Harper & Row, New York.

Levy, C. 1987. Spider and the hummingbird. *Gosse Bird Club Broadsheet* 48:4–5.

Liberty Hyde Bailey Hortorium. 1976. *Hortus third, a concise dictionary of plants cultivated in the U.S. and Canada.* Macmillan Co., New York.

Little, E. L., Jr., R. O. Woodbury, and F. H. Wadsworth. 1974. *Trees of Puerto Rico and the Virgin Islands.* Agriculture Handbook No. 449. U.S. Department of Agriculture, Washington, D.C.

Little, E. L., Jr., and F. H. Wadsworth. 1964. *Common trees of Puerto Rico and the Virgin Islands.* Agriculture Handbook No. 249. U.S. Department of Agriculture, Washington, D.C.

Lodge, G. E. 1896. Notes on some of the West-Indian hummingbirds. *Ibis* 2:495–519.

Miller, J. R. 1978. Notes on birds of San Salvador Island (Watlings), the Bahamas. *Auk* 95:281–87.

Miller, R. S. 1985. Why hummingbirds hover. *Auk* 102(4):722–26.

Mobbs, A. J. 1976. Observations on the Purple-throated Carib Hummingbird. *Avicultural Magazine* 82:196–201.

Morony, J. J., W. J. Bock, and J. Ferrand, Jr. 1975. *Reference list of the birds of the world.* American Museum of Natural History, New York.

Naeem, S., D. S. Dobkin, and B. M. O'Connor. 1985. *Lasioseius* mites *(Acari:Gamasida:Ascidae)* associated with hummingbird-pollinated flowers in Trinidad, West Indies. *International Journal of Entomology* 27(4): 338–53.

News and views. 1965. *Avicultural Magazine* 71:196.

News and views. 1969. *Avicultural Magazine* 75:277.

Northrop, J. I. 1891. The birds of Andros Island, Bahamas. *Auk* 8:73–74.

Oberholser, H. C. 1974. *The bird life of Texas.* Ed. E. B. Kincaid. 2 vols. University of Texas Press, Austin.

Oniki, Y. 1975. Temperatures of some Puerto Rican birds, with note of low temperatures in Todies. *Condor* 77:344.

Owre, O. T. 1976. Bahama Woodstar in Florida: First specimen for continental North America. *Auk* 93:837–38.

Perrins, C., and C. J. O. Harrison. 1979. Reprint. *Birds: Their life, their ways, their world.* Reader's Digest Association, Pleasantville, NY.

Peters, J. L. 1945. *Check-list of birds of the world.* Vol. 5. Harvard University Press, Cambridge, MA.

Pinchon, R. 1976. *Faune des Antilles Françaises: Les Oiseaux.* Imprimerie Bayeusaine, Bayeux, France.

Pinchon, R., and M. Bon Saint-Côme. 1951. Notes et observations sur les oiseaux des Antilles Françaises. *L'Oiseau et la Revue Française d'Ornithologie* 21:4.

Polmar, N., and F. D. Kennedy, Jr. 1981. *Military helicopters of the world.* Naval Institute Press, Annapolis, MD.

Porter, S. 1930. Notes on the birds of Dominica. *Avicultural Magazine* 8:114–21.

Pulich, W. 1968. The occurrence of the Crested Hummingbird, *Orthorhyncus cristatus exilis,* in the United States. *Auk* 85:322.

Raffaele, H. A. 1983. *A guide to the birds of Puerto Rico and the Virgin Islands.* Fondo Educativo Interamericano, San Juan, Puerto Rico.

Raven, P. H. 1973. Why are bird-visited flowers predominantly red? *Evolution* 26(4):674.

Reuther, R. T. 1959. Successful breeding of the Streamertailed Hummingbird. *Avicultural Magazine* 65:103–06.

Reynard, G. B. 1981. *Bird songs in the Dominican Republic.* Cornell Laboratory of Ornithology, phonograph record.

Riba, R., and T. Herrera. 1973. Ferns, lichens, and hummingbirds' nests. *American Fern Journal* 63(3):128.

Ricart, C. 1987. Resource use and feeding ecology of nectar-feeding birds in a lower montane wet forest. M.S. thesis, University of Colorado.

Ridgway, R. 1890. The Hummingbirds. *Report of the U.S. National Museum for 1890,* pp. 253–383.

———. 1911. The birds of North and Middle America. Part V. *Bulletin of the U.S. National Museum* 50:300–601.

Rodiles, I. C. 1960. El Zunzuncito (Pájaro Mosca Cubano). *Sociedad Cubana de Historia Natural* 2:1–7.

Ruschi, A. 1982. *Beija-flores de estado do Espirito Santo.* Editora Rios, São Paulo, Brazil.

Salmon, L. 1972. Jamaican Mango and Red-billed Streamertail. *Gosse Bird Club Broadsheet* 18:23.

Sauer, C. O. 1966. *The early Spanish Main.* University of California Press, Berkeley.

Schreiber, R. W., and E. A. Schreiber. 1984. Mensural and moult data for some birds of Martinique, French West Indies. *Bulletin of the British Ornithological Club* 104(2): 62–68.

Schuchmann, K.-L. 1977. Notes on the display of the Streamertailed Hummingbird *Trochilus polytmus (Lin.). Gosse Bird Club Broadsheet* 28:11–13.

———. 1978. Allopatrische artbildung bei der Kolibrigattung *Trochilus. Ardea* 66:156–72.

———. 1979. Notes on the song, territorial behaviour and the display of the Antillean Crested Hummingbird *Orthorhyncus cristatus exilis* of St. Lucia, W.I. *Bulletin of the British Ornithological Club* 99(1): 30–32.

———. 1980. *Die Jamaika-Kolibris: Trochilus polytmus und Trochilus scitulus.* Biotropic-Verlag, Frankfurt am Main, West Germany.

———. 1988. The birds of the air. *Pacific Discovery* 41(3): 32–39.

Schuchmann, K.-L., and G. Schuchmann-Wegert. 1984. Notes on the displays and mounting behaviour in the Purple-throated Carib Hummingbird *(Eulampis jugularis). Bonn. Zool. Beitr.* 35(4): 327–34.

Severin, T. 1970. *The golden Antilles.* Alfred A. Knopf, New York.

Silva, A. 1982. *Chipojos, bayoyas y camaleones.* Editorial Científico-Técnica, Havana.

Silva, A., and G. Alayon. 1988. *Enciclopedia juvenil: Por los caminos de la edad de oro.* Vol. 12. Editorial Gente Nueva, Havana.

Skutch, A. F. 1964. Life histories of Hermit hummingbirds. *Auk* 81:5–25.

———. 1973. *The life of the hummingbird.* Crown Publishers, New York.

Smith, R. W. 1967. Flight display of the Vervain Hummingbird. *Gosse Bird Club Broadsheet* 8:12–13.

Snow, B. K. 1973. Social organization of the Hairy Hermit *Glaucis hirsuta. Ardea* 61:94–105.

Snow, B. K., and D. W. Snow. 1972. Feeding niches of hummingbirds in a Trinidad valley. *Journal of Animal Ecology* 41:471–85.

Snow, D. W., and B. K. Snow. 1973. The breeding of the Hairy Hermit *Glaucis hirsuta* in Trinidad. *Ardea* 61:106–22.

Spence, S. 1978. Some more notes about Streamertail Hummingbirds. *Gosse Bird Club Broadsheet* 30:8.

Stedman, Mrs. H. 1965. Streamertail Hummingbird. *Gosse Bird Club Broadsheet* 4:20.

Stedman, V. 1974. Nesting habit of female Streamertail. *Gosse Bird Club Broadsheet* 22:20.

Stiles, F. G. 1975. Ecology, flowering phenology, and hummingbird pollination of some Costa Rican *Heliconia* species. *Ecology* 56:285–301.

Stiling, P. D. 1986. *Butterflies and other insects of the eastern Caribbean.* Macmillan Co., New York.

Stimson, L. A. 1944. *Ricordia ricordii* seen at Miami, Florida. *Auk* 61:300.

Sutton, B. 1963. Plants and the birds they attract. *Gosse Bird Club Broadsheet* 4:13.

Taylor, Lady. 1955. *Introduction to the birds of Jamaica.* Macmillan Co., New York.

Tyrrell, E. Q., and R. A. Tyrrell. 1985. *Hummingbirds: Their life and behavior.* Crown Publishers, New York.

Voous, K. H. 1983. *Birds of the Netherlands Antilles.* De Walburg Pers, Utrecht, The Netherlands.

Wells, J. G. 1902. The birds of the island of Carriacou. *Auk* 19(4):344–45.

Wells, J. G., and G. N. Lawrence. 1886. Catalogue of birds of Grenada. *Proceedings of the U.S. National Museum* 9:619–20.

West, R. C., and J. P. Augelli. 1966. *Middle America: Its lands and peoples.* Prentice-Hall, Englewood Cliffs, NJ.

Wetmore, A. 1916a. Birds of Porto Rico. *U.S. Department of Agriculture Bulletin* 326:1–140.

———. 1916b. The birds of Vieques Island, Porto Rico. *Auk* 33:403–19.

———. 1917. Birds of Culebra Island, P.R. *Auk* 34:51–62.

———. 1927. *Scientific survey of Porto Rico and the Virgin Islands.* Vol. 9, Part 4. New York Academy of Sciences.

Wetmore, A., and B. W. Swales. 1931. The birds of Haiti and the Dominican Republic. *Bulletin of the U.S. National Museum* 155:266–76.

Wetmore, A., and F. C. Lincoln. 1933. Additional notes on the birds of Haiti and the Dominican Republic. *Proceedings of the U.S. National Museum* 82(25):1–68.

Wolf, L. L. 1975. "Prostitution" behavior in a tropical hummingbird. *Condor* 77:140–44.

Wolf, L. L., and F. R. Hainsworth. 1971. Time and energy budgets of territorial hummingbirds. *Ecology* 52(6):980–88.

———. 1975. Female territoriality in the Purple-throated Carib. *Auk* 92:511–22.

Wolf, L. L., and J. S. Wolf. 1971. Nesting of the Purple-throated Carib Hummingbird. *Ibis* 113:306–15.

Woods, C. A. 1987. The threatened and endangered birds of Haiti: Lost horizons and new hopes. Paper presented at the Jean Delacour Symposium on Breeding Birds in Captivity. International Foundation for the Conservation of Birds, 12–15 February, at Sheraton Universal Hotel, Universal City, California.

Index

Page numbers in *italics* refer to illustrations.

flycatcher, tyrant, 17, 123
folklore, 107
   see also Indians of Caribbean
food, 164–167
Fork-tailed Hummingbird, *see* Puerto
   Rican Emerald
fossils, 19
Fou-Fou, *see* Antillean Crested
   Hummingbird; Green-throated Carib
Fou-Fou Feuille Blanc, *see* Blue-Headed
   Hummingbird
Fou-Fou Madère, *see* Purple-throated
   Carib
Fou-Fou Tête Longue, *see* Green-throated
   Carib
France, 7
frogs, 15
Frou-Frou, *see* Purple-throated Carib
Frou-Frou Bleu, *see* Blue-headed
   Hummingbird
Frou-Frou Huppé, *see* Antillean Crested
   Hummingbird

Garnet-throated Hummingbird
   (Lamprolaima rhami), 109
genera, of hummingbirds, 17, 19
Gentianaceae, 201, 217
Gesneriaceae, 201–202, 217
Giant Hummingbird, 11
Gilded Sapphire, 11
gizzard, 163
Glaucis, 19, 119
   G. hirsuta, *see* Rufous-breasted Hermit
Glittering Emerald, 11
God Bird, *see* Bahama Woodstar; Cuban
   Emerald
Golden Silk Spider, 15
Gosse, Philip Henry, 151
Gosse Bird Club (Jamaica), *139*
Great Britain, 7
Greater Antilles, 1, 4, 17, 19
Green-backed Firecrown, 9
Green Carib, *see* Green-throated Carib
Green Doctor Bird, *see* Green-throated
   Carib
Green Mango *(Anthracothorax viridis)*,
   11, 17, 78–81, *78, 80, 81,* 167
   courtship of, 80
   description of, 79
   habitat of, 79
   local names of, 79
   measurements of, 79
   mites and, 181
   nectar "robbing" by, 180
   nesting of, 80
   range of, 79
   voice of, 79
   weights of, 79

Green-throated Carib *(Eulampis*
   holosericeus), 14, 17, 82–89, *82, 84,*
   85, 87, 89, 167
   description of, 85
   habitat of, 83, *88*
   local names of, 83
   measurements of, 85
   nesting of, 86, 87
   range of, 83
   voice of, 86
   weights of, 85
Grenada, ix, 4, 19
   Antillean Crested Hummingbirds, 21,
   28
   Green-throated Carib, 83
   Purple-throated Carib, 109
   Rufous-breasted Hermit, 119
Grey Heron, *10*
Gros Colibri, *see* Purple-throated Carib
Guadeloupe, 4
   Purple-throated Carib, 109
Guanahacabibe Indians, 4
Guide to the Birds of Puerto Rico and the
   Virgin Islands, A (Raffaele), 103
Gundlach, Juan, 53, 75
Guttiferae, 202, 217

habitats, 9
   of Antillean Crested Hummingbird, 23
   of Antillean Mango, 37
   of Bahama Woodstar, 43
   of Bee Hummingbird, 53, *61*
   of Blue-Headed Hummingbird, 63, 67
   of Cuban Emerald, 71, 77
   of Eastern Streamertail, 141
   feathers and, 11
   of Green Mango, 79
   of Green-throated Carib, 83, *88*
   of Hispaniolan Emerald, 91, *93*
   of Jamaican Mango, 97, *100*
   of Puerto Rican Emerald, 103
   of Purple-throated Carib, 112
   of Rufous-breasted Hermit, 119, *124,*
   125
   of Vervain Hummingbird, 151
   of Western Streamertail, 127
Hairy Hermit, *see* Rufous-breasted Hermit
Haiti
   Antillean Mango, 35
   Hispaniolan Emerald, 91
   Vervain Hummingbird, 151
Hamelia patens (Scarlet Bush), *61, 208*
hawks, 15, 21
heart rate, 163
Heliconia
   H. bihai (Wild Plantain), *90, 101, 120,*
   124, 125, 183, 184
   H. caribaea (Lobster-claws), *117, 185*

   H. collinsiana, 185
   H. psittacorum (Parrot's Plantain), *31,*
   102, 179, 186
   H. rostrata (Pendant Firebird), *69, 128,*
   149, 179, 187
Heliconiaceae, 183–186
helicopters, hummingbirds compared
   with, 173
"hermits," 12, *13*
Heselton, H. C., 141
hibiscus, *44, 49, 100,* 177
Hibiscus rosa-sinensis, 44, 204
Hispaniola, *see* Dominican Republic; Haiti
Hispaniolan Emerald *(Chlorostilbon*
   swainsonii), x, 17, 90–95, *90, 92, 94,*
   95
   courtship of, 94
   description of, 91–93
   habitat of, 91, *93*
   local names of, 91
   measurements of, 93
   nesting of, *93, 94*
   range of, 91
   voice of, 94
   weights of, 93
Historia naturalis (Pliny), 9
history, of Caribbean, 4, 6
Holmskioldia sanguinea (Japanese Hat),
   159, 213
honey, as food source, 165, *175*
Hoya carnosa, 46
humerus, 164
hummingbirds
   classification of, 9–11
   habitat of, 9
   longevity of, 14
   names of, 11–12
   overview of, 9–15
   physical characteristics of, 12–14
   predators of, 14–15
   range of, 9
   size of, 11
   of world, 219–223
Hurricane Gilbert, 141
hurricanes, ix, 7, 75, 141
hyoid apparatus, 161

Ibis, 97, 109, 127
Ice Age, 19
Indians of Caribbean, 4, 5, 6
insects, 7, 15, 165, 166, 167, *175*
   color and, 177
iridescence, 169–170, *170*
Ixora coccinea (Flame of the Woods), *58,*
   159, 210

Jamaica, ix, x, 4, 6, 7, 15, *19*